A MIRROR ON THE PAST

A MIRROR ON THE PAST

Reflections on a life in the shadow of the mine

DAVID J PARRY

A MIRROR ON THE PAST

First published in 2023.

Copyright © David J Parry 2023.
All paintings Copyright © David J Parry – *www.parrydjpics.com*

David J Parry has asserted his rights under the Copyright, Designs and Patents Act 1988
to be identified as the author of this work.

A CIP catalogue record for this book is available from the British Library.

ISBN: 978-1-3999-5285-9

All rights reserved. No part of this book covered by the copyright herein may be reproduced or used in any form or by any means – graphic, electronic, or mechanised, including photocopying, recording, taping or information storage and retrieval systems – without the written permission of David J Parry.

Every effort has been made to obtain the necessary permissions with reference to copyright material, both illustrative and quoted. We apologise for any omissions in this respect and will be pleased to make the appropriate acknowledgements in any future edition.

Design and production by Ryder Design – *www.ryderdesign.studio*

Front cover: **Wharncliffe Woodmoor Disaster 1936**. Acrylic on canvas. © David J Parry.

CONTENTS

Author's Note vi
Acknowledgments vii
Foreword ix

1 Pit work 1
2 Finding my 'pit legs' 19
3 Through the glass – 'The past we inherit.' 27
4 "Hearts that loved never forget." 35
5 Early days – growing up and getting out 47
6 Blurred visions and conflict 59
7 "Take prisoners!" – the battles at Orgreave 73
8 Fighting like girls 89
9 Against all the odds – hanging on 99
10 Returning to work and rebuilding the NUM branch .. 123
11 Facing up to closure 143
12 The future we build 151
13 Privatisation, the long goodbye and
    coalfield communities 165
14 Walking this road together – and alone 183

Postscript 206

Wash Day Blues (poem) 207
Two Seven Five (poem) 208
On Firth Three (poem) 209
Tears and Fears (poem) 210

Glossary 211

AUTHOR'S NOTE

When I started writing this book, in 2016, I made up a character – near enough me – but not necessarily me. I wanted the book to be about a particular period of history told from first-hand experience. Yes, it's my story but it is also 'our' story.

Having read the manuscript, friends advised me it would read better in the first person and I have redrafted it accordingly. The 'I' in the book may indeed be me but the story largely relays the life experiences of those around me. It is, I hope, the story that is important, not who tells it.

This book contains reflections of a former coalminer from South Yorkshire. I was part of the last generation of my wider family to work in a coal mine. My great grandparents moved from Mostyn Quay Colliery in North Wales in the early 1880s to work the mines in South Yorkshire.

Around 1.2 million people were employed in the industry in 1920. At the time of nationalisation in 1947 some 960 collieries employed over 700,000 miners. The last deep mine in the UK was closed in December 2015.

This book makes no attempt to be comprehensive and is based on memory, some personal diary entries, and previous written material. It is personal and selective in many ways.

It is not meant to be a forensically detailed account and some 'artistic licence' is taken. It attempts to convey and reflect, not just events but an authentic sense of a particular part of history from one participant's viewpoint. If there are any important historical inaccuracies, they are not deliberate, merely the result of the passage of time.

The publication is not a commercial venture and I am not seeking any literary recognition. It is an interpretation as well as a record and stands as it is.

The detailed descriptive sections on coal mining may be difficult to grasp, but please try. The footnotes and glossary should help.

ACKNOWLEDGMENTS

Most of the acknowledgments can be found in the extensive footnotes. It's not done with academic rigour.

I do have some acknowledgments of omission. Not because of any lack of significance, but because the focus of the story is elsewhere. First of all, for my family and friends. Secondly, to the women activists in the strike and later – whose story is better told by the women involved than me.

FOREWORD

Reflecting now … and then.

A glance in the mirror – there is some doubt now, some background anxiety – life goes on. So many blind alleys and missed opportunities. Just get on with it.

Mirrors can be tricky things. A window on another world? Perhaps telling the truth, but sometimes also distorting or hiding the truth. The reflection is always in reverse – right and left switched. Can they be trusted? 'Smoke and mirrors' are the stock-in-trade of politicians and second-hand car salesmen – half-truths, illusions and downright lies.

Now you see it – now you don't!

We have all the best intentions but then come up short.

We look but don't see. We think we see, yet haven't really looked.

Check your mirrors.

Pitscape. Acrylic on canvas. © David J Parry.

Shearer on a Run. Acrylic on canvas. © David J Parry.

1

PIT WORK

Lords of the coal face
Kings of the Underworld[1]

Arms outstretched, I reach the switch and flick on the light beside the bed. Briefly dazed, I throw off the covers, stand and stub my toes on the chest of drawers as I make my way across the bedroom. The offending furniture is given a death stare. The darkness, now lit by 40 watts, begins to make sense and I now know what to do next. Not quite on autopilot but still, a very familiar ritual awaits, practised time and time again. But obviously not enough, hence the stubbed toe. This is what is known as the day shift, but it feels like the middle of the night.

But what day? Oh yes – Tuesday. Where was Monday? Where was the weekend? Days away now – unconsciously wishing away my life as I dress myself.

Downstairs now and another switch – more light. Then another switch – this time the kettle. The first noise of the day. A cup of instant coffee, no time to faff around and make a decent cup. Yet it does the trick and eases a dry throat.

---

1 Richard Burton speaking in: *Every Valley*, Public Service Broadcasting. 2017.

No breakfast – can't be arsed.

Sliced brown bread, bit of marg' and cheese are thrown together to make snap[2] and stuffed in an old plastic bread bag. That's about it … money? ……… keys?

The back door clicks shut and the cold air hits my face and hands. The frosted windscreen was not on the 'to do' list. Minimising time and effort was essential when only half the body and half the mind are working properly at five in the morning. Now it's another unplanned fuck about. Scrape up, then down, then maybe across. A bit more here and a bit more there – it'll have to do. The old car kicks into life and I let it run for a minute or two as I adjustment the fan for the screen.

Driving carefully now through the back streets glistening with frost in the headlights. Am I the only person daft enough to be out and about at this time of day? No, a taxi passes and a dark figure shuffles across the road at the end of the street. So many different ways to get to work, but in the winter, it's best to stick to main roads.

Twenty minutes later the spotlight from No2 shaft winding gear spreads a fierce beam across the pit yard and dark figures move around, all drawn to this gathering. Some coming and some going. The noise of starter motors kicking cold engines to life can be heard above the drone of the pit fan house.

The shift changeover is a brief chance to talk to workmates – even if some of them are definitely not your mates.

"Mornin' … mornin', mornin.'"

"Heyup Jack! How tha gooin?"

"Fair to middling considering."

"How've yer gone on?"

Jack now has his chance for a dig: "Well, we've done nowt but we've made sure you lot can!"

Beneath a thick layer of sarcasm, what he means is S01s face has been broken down most of the night shift. The main coal face shearer had been tested to destruction and ground to a halt. The usual fate of most machinery in coal mines. These machines are built in sections and it's usually easier to remove

---

2 Food/snack for underground consumption. Also known as 'bait' in the North East.

the knackered section rather than trying to repair it on the coal face. But it's still a big job getting the old section off and transporting a new section along a face with barely enough clearance to crawl.

Inevitably there is lots of casual effing and blinding but finding someone to blame isn't easy. Arse kicking usually starts at the top and comes down the ranks. Thankfully, management and supervisors have learned they have to be careful when trying to pass on the blame to members of the NUM. The overman, control room on the surface and the under-manager exchange nervous phone calls every ten minutes, but, step by step, the new haulage section is fitted to Number 1 machine. A shiny brass plaque tells us it was made in Motherwell by Anderson Strathclyde. All being well, there is nothing stopping the next shift from whipping off four or five strips and putting a smile back on the face of management.

Coming on shift there is some silver lining to this particular cloud. Cutting coal makes the time go much quicker. During long break-downs, every minute creeps along, dragging out the shift, unless of course you have to sort out the breakdown. Fitters, electricians, overmen and managers all prefer the job to run smoothly.

Glum faces file past the time office window. One glance and eye contact made, two brass checks are passed to you. He knows who you are even if you are a bit hazy about who he is. One round and one octagonal, each stamped with a number and embossed with the colliery name. Pit checks are you. They are not a substitute or a version of you – they are you. An identity that logs you in, without which you do not exist in the here and now. A number means very little – unless it's the number on your pit check.

Decades later a dream returned time and time again. It found me arriving at the pit bottom and realising I had not taken my checks out. Panic set in as I pondered what to do: phone the time office and explain? Wing it and hope for the best? Then I also might realise I had no helmet or one boot missing and in confusion and disbelief everything spiralled out of control. I thought it was shift work that disturbed my sleep pattern but long after I left the pit, sleep was hit and miss for me.

Canteen first. Another coffee, if you have time. It gets a bit more sociable between the still bleary-eyed individuals squinting under the glaring strip lighting and the banter starts to pick up. Some night shift men are waiting for a pit bus – they are happy enough to be getting off home but you have no motivation to smile, just a grim resignation to get on with it. A glance at the clock on the wall tells you to do just that: get on with it.

Clean side – rows of galvanised lockers double decked. Blokes at various stages of undress. That smell. The smell of coal and dirt subjected to soap and water. Strangely, I remember it from being a kid; when mother was washing my father's pit clothes. A grey scum in the washer, moving across the surface of the water, popping soap bubbles. A plume of steam drifting across the kitchen.

A locker key is part of the essential kit and it too has a number. Bollock-naked with a towel, a soap bag and your snap, you walk unselfconsciously up the locker bays and take a 90-degree turn to the mucky side.

Opening your locker door, the smell of coal and dirt intensifies as you pick out your pit clobber. Having not taken anything home to wash and not put your orange overalls in to be laundered, you have to wear last week's clothes. Boots are a bit curled up but then the lockers are warm. Pit checks are clipped to the belt along with the locker key. A first aid pouch is also attached to the belt. Knee pads need slackening off at the top strap and then helmet on, snap in top pocket, water bottle and onwards. Bottle filled at the taps above a row of sinks. Passing through the boot room where some lads are having a last fag.

Across the yard is the lamp cabin where you pick up your cap lamp, fit the battery to your belt and wrap the cable loosely around the neck. Clipping the cap lamp to your helmet comes later when you'll need two hands. Onto the belt goes a shiny self-rescuer. The device converts poisonous carbon monoxide to carbon dioxide for about an hour and a half – after that you're in deep shit. A couple of disposable dusts mask are shoved in your pocket and you walk to the air lock for Number 2 shaft.

It's 5.50 in the morning and the light is just beginning to break over the tip to the east. Contraband zone – each miner on the oncoming shift is casually frisked for anything that may produce a spark. Battery operated watches, for example, are contraband. Then it's into the airlock[3]. Steel doors are opened

---

3 Airlock/air doors: to prevent ventilation short-circuiting – provides a positive airflow from one shaft around the workings and then up the other shaft(s).

with some effort and then closed before another set open. The rush of air whips around trying to short-circuit between two areas of pressure. You now stand on the pit bank[4] and it's the upcast shaft[5], so a fair bit warmer than outside. This air has been miles around the underground workings picking up heat, dust and gases before being sucked to the surface by a huge fan.

Steel ropes whizz up and down and the background roar of the passing air makes conversation a struggle. Les, the banksman, smiles but gets little joy from the assembled crowd. No helmet, he hasn't a hair out of place due to the copious application of 'Brylcreem'. Playing host to the glum souls, he has a word for everyone and talks fast as though commentating on the run-in of a horse race. A stand-up comic who has missed his calling cracking jokes at pace, skipping around the lines of miners.

His bumptiousness, however, goes largely unrewarded as each man hands him a round brass check and steps onto the cage. A mesh gate closes them in and, sardine-like, the men stand waiting for the banksman to signal to the winder. Farting is not appreciated at such close quarters, but then neither is garlic.

Dropping now. Two decks packed and travelling against the air, the noise builds with speed. Each man has his own cap lamp but no one uses it and the only break in the dark descent is the flash of lights as the cage passes pump lodges in the shaft. Then the cage slows dramatically and a bit of g-force comes into play. The last few feet are nice and easy as the brightly lit pit bottom comes into view. After plummeting over 2000 feet, the cage comes to a halt.

Clunk, slam, then crash, the wire mesh is lifted and men step out past the onsetter into a different world. This is a place where dirty whitewash is the colour scheme of choice and there is twenty feet of headroom with strip lighting. But it's only the first stage in the underground journey. There's a few more miles yet and quite a lot deeper to go.

Diving on to the bottom belt of the man-rider conveyor, I shuffle around to get comfy, re-arranging the bits and pieces on my belt. I am carried down the return drift to the Swallow Wood seam on a rubber carpet – another 350 feet of descent in a roadway of about 1:4. Here there is more strip lighting and

---

4 The area around a shaft top where men and materials etc. are loaded and unloaded.
5 See footnote 3 – the shaft taking air out of the mine.

a bustle of activity as men go in different directions. The team assemble and climb onto the low-slung paddy train[6] and before long are rattling along the tailgate in pitch black, save for the loco headlights. The coal face is still about 2000 metres away. The air is warm and moist but there's not much dust because of the overnight breakdown. There is some conversation but mind and body have yet to get going and the screeching of the paddy wheels and roar of the diesel loco drown most of the chat.

Arriving inbye [7] there is still another 50 metres to amble forward in a roadway set with 14 feet by 12 feet arched girders. This is the tail gate or supply gate. In my time down the pit, coal faces were either advanced or retreat. Faces typically consisted of two parallel roadways about 150–300 metres apart with the coal face itself running at 90 degrees between the two roadways. The main gate or loader gate brings access and air to the face and is usually the route out for the coal conveyor. The tail gate makes a circuit by taking away the stale air, and provides the main supply of materials route.

On an advanced face the roadways are built incrementally, steel arch by steel arch, as the face itself advances. This is known as ripping. On a retreat face the roadways are pre-driven and the face itself retreats back down the two roadways already in place. This has the advantage of divorcing coal production from roadway development. If planned properly, it's a much more effective way of mining coal. On an advanced face there are too many activities taking place at the same time, often interrupting production.

Dropping on the knees, the cutting team crawl through the pack hole onto the face then crawl along the chock track on autopilot. They are working just less than five feet of coal, but with heavy-duty supports and kit, there's not much room for humans. Crawling or bunny hopping is about all you can manage.

I'm most likely the only one to look around – squinting with one eye down the face pan line[8] trying to log any misalignment I may need to correct

---

6 A small train, either rope-hauled or diesel-powered, for transporting underground workers.
7 Inbye is the farthest point of any underground district from shafts. Outbye is the area nearer the shafts.
8 The steel conveyor running along a face is constructed of sections (pans) bolted together but not rigid, with a scraper chain running in a race top and bottom.

at some point during the shift. My key job – 'snaker' – was lining up 250m of armoured face conveyor. The machine man's key job is making sure the cutting horizon[9] is spot on. Getting both of these jobs done correctly saves a lot of potential trouble from roof falls and reduces wear and tear on machinery.

When this face was first installed, around 1982, the main machine was fitted with an automatic steering device. It employed a nucleonic sensor that read the different levels of radiation emitted from coal and stone. Optimally, it should have steered the disc to cut about two or three inches from the seam roof. Despite the best efforts of a pack of technical staff from Area HQ, the machine repeatedly lost its bearings and would start either mining out the floor too far or cutting the top out. Consequently, the device was taken out and the face went back to manual controls relying on the skills of the machine operator. Such steering mechanisms were successfully introduced when the software of new information technology came into its own later in the 1990s.

Automatically steering a coal-face shearer and steering a panzer[10] over 200m long was beyond the technology of the time. Coal faces are not factory floors, but a natural environment, millions of years old. Seams of coal follow the contours of pre-history. Getting thousands of tonnes of stupid, brainless metal to do the same is not always straightforward.

The eerie quiet is broken abruptly by the face panzer alarm and the heavy 'clunketty-clunk' of the face chain on the move. With the flip of a brass handle, the main machine springs into life with renewed vigour after its overnight refurb. It's a single-ended ranging drum shearer. It has an electric motor driving a series of hydraulic pumps to operationalise the power, cutting the coal and traversing the face. One disc is normally all that is needed in five feet of coal, but double-ended shearers are common in thicker seams. The disc dictates the height and depth of cut but it can be ranged up and down on an arm. Some older machines had hydraulic jacks to alter the cutting horizon.

---

9   Cutting the coal at an optimum distance from the stone roof.
10 Panzer: armored flexible conveyor. Name derives from the German tank.

A spiral of tungsten-tipped picks do the destructive work, cutting and pushing the coal on to the face conveyor.

Water on the picks and off it goes, dragging itself along the hauler chain like a demented bulldog, cutting disc smashing everything in its way to smithereens. Dust and noise lets the rest of the cutting team know they also need to get into action.

The shearer is well in front now as I squeeze the ram handle and the panzer snakes easily over. I look along to the machine through the thick dust, then back behind.

'Ok ... fine ... a touch more, that'll do it,' I assure myself despite limited vision in the dust.

Scurrying from pan side to the chocks[11] I lock one ram on and, crouching in the adjacent chock, I lower the face support with a crack. Pulling now, not shoving, the chock 'walks' forward and showers me in grains of dirt and coal shards. This cloud of dust quickly joins all the other clouds coming from moving machinery and falling ground and whips away in a blinding vortex pulled through the long narrow face before slowing as it reaches the much higher tail gate, where it hangs in the air like a mist.

Hiss, then thump, then crunch – I set the chock in the advanced position and take another glance at the panzer alignment and, keeping an eye on the roof of the newly exposed ground behind the shearer in front of me, I bunny hop along to repeat the exercise. The rest of the team follow on, bringing all the other supports forward and starting a rolling thunder as the ground behind – better known as the gob[12] – breaks and adds to the cacophony.

This form of mining is sometimes known as 'long-wall' or 'complete cave in'. No attempt is made to support the roof behind the face, except in the roadways. As the face moves forward all the weight of mother earth is supposed

---

11 Chocks: Hydraulically operated face supports consisting of base and telescopic legs with a steel canopy. A horizontal ram is used to push the conveyor forward (sometimes back) and drag/advance the support into a new position after the coal is cut.
12 The area behind a face that is allowed/encouraged to collapse.

to fall behind into the gob. As a strip of coal is removed at the front, stone falls behind the face supports. Or is supposed to. Sometimes it hangs about and sometimes it breaks up in front of the face – bad news. That is why face alignment really matters. If I wanted to be an annoying smart arse when asked what I did for a living, I might answer, 'Strata Control Engineer'.

The fall of ground behind the working area is normal but sometimes a little alarming. When the gob doesn't break, as the mining process carries on, the weight builds up. Then there can be a huge collapse of ground that sounds not unlike an avalanche. Bang – whoosh, a shockwave screams past down the face sucking the air with it and then dust envelopes everything. It stops you in your tracks and, for a second or two, you wonder if someone or something deep in the earth has got it in for you.

After a 150m of this long-wall process, the machine bursts into the main gate[13] hissing and spitting jets of water as the disc now spins freely in open space. Water off (it's bad form to flood the area where men will have to work). Traversing the machine in the opposite direction, it runs over the cowl and the machine starts taking another bite of coal. This is known in management jargon as a 'bi–di' or bi-directional cut. Another way of achieving the same result is to ram the spinning coal cutting disc directly into the coal – known as 'sumping' in.

The last chock to advance is about 20m from the main gate and I crawl past the machine and driver to the gate side as it comes towards me. Once the disc is taking a full cut again, the machine man buries the disc in the floor and runs back over the cowl ready to take another bite of coal at the main gate end of the face. With a gloved finger on a Tannoy button, looking up and back, I shout into the mic inside the steel box: "Ready to ram over?"

The stage loader operator in the gate replies, "Ram when ready!"

A second or two lapses then the gear head[14] judders, then lurches forward

---

13 The intake roadway, which also takes the coal away on a rubber conveyor.
14 The delivery end of a face conveyor with one or two powerful motors.

as face and gate rams push and pull in unison. The main gate end slides forward with all its attached machinery on the Pan-Technicon sliding along the monorail. Tonnes and tonnes of kit edging forward.

'Bit tight that … ' I'm thinking. I pause and glance up and down the panzer … 'Fuck it, I'll straighten up on the way out … '

The machine repeats its pass into and out of the main gate. It's now on the 'big run' to the tail gate. Another ram over at the gear head and supports are brought in to tighten up and hold the new ground. The cycle is complete. The rippers can now advance the roadway and keep up with face. Plenty of time to go – it's a good start to the shift.

"Yeeahhh!" screeches the machine man like an extra in a Western cow-punching in the dust. The shearer drags its fearsome disc relentlessly along, smashing and grinding the coal seam onto the panzer as a broad stream of coal makes its way on the long trip to the surface. The roaring of the machine and the choreographed movement of panzer and face supports continue unabated. Everything is on the move as coal and stone clash with heavy-duty machinery.

Then, in an instant, the panzer stops and as coal piles up behind the driver stops the machine and silences the hissing water jets.

"Snap time … NUM members and others … " announces the stage loader[15] attendant after waiting for a bit of quiet. The 'others' are supervisory staff and taking the piss is routine. 'One a day' was often uttered by colliers in the presence of an overman. This apparently innocuous remark, meant as a threat to execute one overman a day in reprisal for all their wrongs. Humour often has its dark side, especially in male workplaces.

The team set another three or four chocks just to keep things tight and then we settle down for twenty minutes break. Now that the dust has settled, I can look back down the panzer. 'Jobs a good un,' I reassure myself, then slump onto a bed of dirt and coal in the chock track. No snap – I ate that coming inbye. Carrying food around on a coal face doesn't appeal for some reason. The face team are all tucked up a little way behind the shearer as Gurner gets his big stainless-steel flask of coffee out and everyone gets

---

15 A steel conveyor attached at a right angle to the face conveyor to take coal to the main roadway conveyor.

a slurp or two. Gurner got his nickname from having none of his own teeth. He has another epithet – Bela Lugosi – on account of him being 'buried more times than Dracula'.

Gurner has either no nerves or no brains. He would timber up cavities above the face supports as if he were sitting in his own living room. The fact that he was often buried in small falls of ground, the odd annoying scrape and cut, seemed to be his calling. Yet falls of ground are what often kill.

Much of the heavy work of the coal face since the 1970s is done by various machines. Electrical power, hydraulic power and sometimes compressed air power, all play a role in the assault on a subterranean landscape last seen millions of years ago. But machines can't do everything and some of the most dangerous work on a coalface is done, as it always has been, by colliers putting themselves in harm's way.

A fall of ground on a face can range from a few inches thick and a couple of metres along, to sky-high cavities along sections of the coal face. A coal face cannot progress through broken ground – the roof, wherever it is above the face, requires support. The only people capable and daft enough to work in a cavity building a support structure are coal-face workers.

Another feature of falls of ground is buried machinery, including the hydraulic face supports or chocks. Don't let anyone tell you they don't use shovels in a modern coal mine; it's the only tool that can do the job. Known affectionately as 'idiot sticks', shovels come to the rescue time and time again.

The work done in a fall of ground or cavity is done in silence – ears pricked and eyes out on stalks. A tiny stream of dirt particles falling from above is enough to have the men dive for cover. False alarm? Near miss? They're all part of the cat-and-mouse game played with lumps of stone the size of a fridge freezer.

This morning the face is behaving itself. More silence, then the earth groans again and the gob breaks thirty metres back up the face and another cloud of dust rushes past. A hand is quickly placed over the coffee cup to protect it from the grey swirling particles. Silence once more. The team chat about some crap on the television or perhaps football – any old shit to take your mind off work.

A light bobs up and down and side to side coming from the tail gate. It's the district deputy on his rounds. He is affectionately known as Water Buffalo because of his habit of drinking everybody else's water but not carrying his own. He informs the team they are likely to be stood outside the tail gate. There's been some cock up with supplies for the pack hole and the rip will be out of bounds if another cut or shear is taken. This would leave too much unsupported roof. So much for getting four strips off…

"Want a bit up?" a chocker asks the deputy.

"Don't mind if I do," the deputy replies, taking a pinch of snuff from the opened tin in front of him. He slumps on his backside and savours the moment. His eyes water a little as the menthol circulates in his airways.

It's a peculiar habit but taking snuff is a little social ritual common to coal miners. Brown snot is the down side and only the really addicted take it in 'polite' company outside the workplace. Chewing tobacco is also common with smokers and brown spit is not very appealing either. Snuff and chewing tobacco came with added 'flavours' such as aniseed. I tried it from time to time but taking snuff from your mates and not buying a tin was frowned upon.

The Tannoy bursts into life with a message for the deputy – he is wanted in the main gate. Then another message – a setting of wood chocks is needed for the gate side as soon as possible after snap. The tail gate rippers hear the message but take no heed. They have plenty to do without loading the face conveyor with timber. Cursing their interrupted snap time the timber lad and tail gate supervisor combine to fetch the requested chock wood. The twenty minutes are up and the panzer creaks and groans into motion. With the timber nestling between the flight bars, it slides under the face machines and makes is way to the main gate.

The main machine remains silent, the operator waiting for the word to start again. The main gate rippers have got their timber and the machine is kicked into life once more as it continues its journey towards the tail gate, dragging its disc and ploughing coal onto the conveyor like a black stream. Arriving 30 metres from the tail end of the face, I push and twist the key on the face signals and the panzer stops.

"Lock out at tail gate!" informs the stage loader attendant over the Tannoy.

"What's up?" asks another voice. It's the Control Room on the surface, all dust free and cosy.

"Like fucking lightning, these pillocks," mutters Gurner as he spits out a reply: "Stood waiting for tail gate shearer … "

"Why?" asks the Control Room

"You were told nearly an hour ago we are out of bounds with the rip![16]" chimes in the deputy.

"Oh … it's just that we have an ops manager[17] in 15s heading[18] and he wants to know … " answers the Control Room attendant apologetically.

"We will let you know," replies the deputy through gritted teeth. He softens his face and slowly smiles like a long-lost uncle.

"Okey-dokey … steady as she goes … " The deputy shuffles off on his knees, a one-man patrol.

The gate side pack[19] is now on and face side leg set so the tail gate shearer cuts in and out again with main machine gliding into the open track and turning the cowl once more to begin a run back along the face. Closing up the supports behind, the rest of the face team wait as the main machine drags on the hauler chain and starts another cut.

I inform the machine man, "It's a bit tight around 120 chock – the face was getting behind."

"Pillock," comes the reply. "We've lost enough time already!"

Mm … *'pillock' is it?* – I think to myself – *I suppose it will be pillock when we have to straighten the face up tomorrow and lose bonus.* Productivity bonus is based on linear metres cut and also depth of cut or advance. Straightening up

---

16 The distance between last arch support set and the coal face is greater than Management Support Rules.
17 Operations Manager from Area NCB level.
18 Mining operation in a new roadway for development of a coal face.
19 Pack – thick column of stone or wood to help support the roadway.

bent faces makes good mining sense but doesn't add to the bonus pot. This tension was a running sore and often didn't win me any friends.

In full flow at first, then slowing in the tight track, the machine grinds off the coal, bouncing and bucking as it snatches on the hauler chain. The hauler chain runs the full length of the face and is anchored at each end. One blow from it as it thrashes and bounces up and down and side to side would easily take your head off.

Inch by inch the machine forces its way through and then, reaching a wider track, surges forward and picks up more speed again. The machine driver's irritation subsides as there is still a good chance of four strips. No hold ups now as the cycle of cutting coal following up with face supports along the 250 metres face is repeated.

The coal flows warm and wet from machine picks to panzer, to conveyors, to the pit bottom bunker, up the shaft in skips, yet more conveyors, coal preparation plant, loading pad, then train or truck to the steel works or coke ovens or – in small amounts – for domestic use.

Returning late in the shift for the third time to the main gate, the machine man stops, turns the water off, then turns and takes out the brass handle on the machine. A few more supports are moved forward and extension arms run out behind the now silent coal shearer. That's OK, not too tight. Back down the face the last chocker in the team is also tightening up. 'Job's a good 'un.'

"That's it, let some other fucker take over," I murmur to myself. This relief is shared by all as the team spill out into the main gate, standing up for first time in several hours.

We walk down the gate to the back of the transformers slung on monorails before diving onto the conveyor belt. This part is not legal but, as they say, third class riding is better than first class walking any day. Sharp-eyed and alert to snags and dangers and keeping well down, the team squeeze under deformed arches with the belt high in the roadway. Swinging from steel slings holding the conveyor they each find a way back off and march up the cross gate before once again diving onto a conveyor – this time a man-riding conveyor so less caution is required.

We pass the afternoon shift coming the other way. The blackened faces with the contrasting white smiles are full of banter and well-meaning insults for the clean-faced on comers. Some useful information about the job is also exchanged, but no time to hang about for most.

Pit bottom again but this time going in the right direction: up. A wait now as each cage is loaded and rapped to bank. Eager beavers jostle for position.

I have no interest in the scrum to get on the cage; I am happy to be on the last pull. After all, I will be calling in at the union office so my shift is not quite over. There is an important meeting with management later in the week – important for whom is another question.

The onsetter leans over the big metal gate and informs me the operations manager who had been visiting 15s development had gone ape-shit. The heading is a basket case, so they say, and there's no chance the next face will be ready in time.

"Heard it all before," I quietly respond.

"We've told 'em often enough, they should have started it months ago. You could see a production gap staring you in the fuckin' face. Anyway, with a bit of luck the bonus will be OK – at least for a while. See you tomorrow."

The wire curtain drops to ankle height and soon I'm winging my way upwards.

Arriving at the pit bank I hand my second brass check to the banksman. He struggles to keep up with the flow of men intent on getting off shift as soon as possible and drops a couple on the concrete floor. Still taking my time, I emerge into the fresh air at the back of the pack.

Now then – shower and change first or straight up to the union office? I hesitate for a second or two, then opt for the shower. The rest of the shift are scrambling through the pit baths half washed – who gives a shit about a bit of a tide mark around the neck? Going home, going to the pub – anywhere but here!

The showers are fairly quiet as I start to lather up the bar of Pit Head Baths (PHB) soap – a green slab with caustic properties. Splat! A big sponge hits me between the shoulders and I am given a carwash treatment by a fellow miner. Squinting round through stinging soap I see that it's Steve, a fitter from the headings. The sponge flips – scourer side now.

"Steady on for Christ's sake, my back'll be red raw!" I whinge.

This gets a wicked laugh from the fitter but now I have to return the favour. Washing each other's back is normal practice in pit baths – who else is going to do it? Unfortunately for me, Steve's back is twice the size of my own so I don't get much of a fair deal.

Changed in to civvies, dripping wet hair, I wander over the pit yard to catch two union colleagues who are sitting at Formica tables, a few shabby files in front of them and the smell of fags ingrained into every crevice in the office.

Arriving at pit bank. Acrylic on canvas.

© David J Parry.

2

FINDING MY 'PIT LEGS'

Eventually, I became more comfortable with the job, confident in my abilities and a familiar figure. But when I first started at Thurcroft pit early in 1977, it was all a bit different. I had done manual jobs but never learned a skill. Despite the long-haired 'hippy' image, I usually fitted in and tried not to rock the boat. Coal mining is way out of most people's comfort zone, but I wasn't fazed. I had to complete basic training, which involved visiting an old hand-filled face training gallery at the soon to close Orgreave Colliery. I particularly remember the magnificent steam winding engine with affection.

Then, in a yellow helmet under Close Personal Supervision (CPS) of one of the older colliers, I first worked for the safety team collecting airborne dust samples for the NCB Area laboratories. Mainly this training involved getting used to the environment and avoiding silly injuries. Haulage, or underground transport is, in many ways, more dangerous than face work and there is a lot to learn. My first regular job was at a remote junction where one conveyor fed the coal and dirt onto another – a 'button' job. It was a new development to open up a face in the Haigh Moor seam. That same development broke the European record for metres advanced in a week. Soon after, there was a major fall of ground and it took weeks to get back on schedule.

From time to time, I picked up a shovel and cleaned up some mineral spillage. There was a little seat tucked into the 'gate' side out of the cold intake air where I read books that I illegally stashed in my donkey coat pocket. The time went very slowly and I yearned for something more interesting to do.

I spent most of the shift on my own with two visits from the district deputy doing his rounds. Behind him was H02s[20] old main gate. It was not sealed off, but it was not a travelling road. It was a useful place to take a dump in now and then. I could have gone for a very long walk if I felt like it but might end up asphyxiated. A deputy manager had done just that some years before and although suicide was a possibility, it was never proven.

Thankfully, after six months I was sent to a nearby colliery, Silverwood, to get face-trained. My time-keeping was a 100 per cent so I gave them no excuses to hold me back. I hadn't got a job at the pit just to sit on my arse thousands of yards from the rest of humanity. I went onto a production face assigned for area training. About five trainees from South Yorkshire pits were paired up with colliers on the face itself or in the ripping and pack holes at either end. It meant working a week-about on the various jobs, picking up the knowledge and experience needed. The supervising colliers had an easy time allowing the young trainees to do most of the work. This face was nicknamed the 'Lazy Acre' by other faceworkers at the pit because, with five trainees per shift, in addition to standard manning, the workload was much less.

After 100 days training, I returned to my own pit and worked in the developments on what was called 'improvership' – another 30 days extra training in heading work. This meant driving tunnels to open up other faces. At the time, the team I was sent to was opening up a retreat face using square work – rectangular instead of arched tunnels.

A Dosco Dintheader was used to cut out the ground in-seam. It was my first experience of this type of machine, having only worked on advancing face units. When there were no officials around, the machine driver gave me

---

20 Faces were given letters and numbers for identification and coal seam. In this case H stands for Haigh Moor. Seams are often named from where they outcrop – in this case Haigh (Northwest of Barnsley).

the controls of the machine from time to time. It wasn't officially part of the training; training on cutting machines came later for faceworkers once they had more experience. A Dintheader is a wide, tracked machine with a big broad pick mat on a jib that could be lowered or raised to the appropriate position for cutting or indeed setting steel bars. Three big bites of the machine, taking about a foot of dirt floor as well as the coal seam, usually did the job. RSJ-type girders are set with 7ft-high legs and another cut made.

I worked with big Archie, a near-silent Scot who was bald but covered in thick body hair. He seemed to revel in all the heavy work and had no interest in the machine. At work in a hot, sticky, dusty heading, he wore a helmet with cap lamp, belt with battery and self-rescuer and boots. No socks, no vest and definitely no shorts or underwear. How he kept his dick out of trouble was a wonder.

By this time, I was now a trained-up face worker, paid the highest hourly rate in the industry and expected to tackle everything I was deployed to do. After a few weeks in the pit face 'market' – filling in when other face workers didn't turn up – I was deployed on a job in a face 'stable hole'[21]. It was my first regular face job but it was not one I had not done in training because it was considered old fashioned on modern coal faces.

There was a loud thud and then deathly quiet. The air was now thick with smoke, dust and a sickly smell – powder reek. The smoke swirled and rushed along the face towards the tail end with a strong pull of the ventilation circuit. Before it had all cleared, I scurried back to the face entrance and peered over the face conveyor to look at the handiwork. The view of a huge pile of steaming coal emerged from the murk.

Not at all bad, that should be about enough … oops wait a minute … there's a Dowty prop[22] missing from under the first bar. I look again, this time

---

21 Area mined, in seam, at the end of a face to allow the advance and turn round of the coal face shearer. Usually requiring boring and firing of coal, hand filling and props and bars set to support the new roof.
22 A type of manually operated hydraulic prop.

with a little less self-congratulatory feeling. I spot it tucked under the gear head on the stage loader – blown out by the blast. More urgency needed – I lock the conveyors out with a twist of the key.

"Prop on stage loader ... seems OK. Just let it run into the gate," I inform my workmates.

The lock-out is taken off and the two armoured conveyors spring into life in turn. Coal streams along the stage loader and a main gate ripper lifts the stray prop from the conveyor and dumps it unceremoniously on the floor. The ripper looks half-threatening, half-laughing and utters the timeless compliment: "Useless pillocks."

The 'pillocks' in question pick up the prop and return it to the face, lock out the face conveyor, throw it over onto the face side, with the shovel dig out a space in the pile of coal, find the floor and set the prop. Now quickly they follow up with other Dowty props as they move the steel bars holding the roof to cover the newly exposed ground. All nice and tight, 0.9 metres apart.[23] Now they can let the armoured conveyors go again and everybody else on the unit can get on with the business of cutting coal.

The 'stable hole' was for the cutting machine – not a pit pony. The job, with two mates, was to bore and fire (blow up) about five metres of coal at sufficient forward depth, then cover our backs in the newly exposed ground with old fashioned props and bars. The borer was compressed-air powered and we used a drill about a metre long to start the hole. It was then extended with a drill about two metres in length. The boring pattern was crucial to achieve the correct end result.

Annoyingly, I was identified by mates, only half-jokingly, as a secret agent and given the nickname Dick Barton – Special Agent, after a 1950s radio programme. It re-emerged as a television programme in the 1970s. The hero saved the nation from disaster time and time again in the fifteen-minute episodes. I was no such hero. I must have been a bit of a mystery to my mates, not really fitting the profile of a pit lad. As far they knew I was another 'green' recruit with no pit history. I had long curly hair, no tattoos, didn't smoke fags and the beer belly didn't arrive until many years later.

---

23 *Management Support Rules* are strictly applied for each face or heading.

In some circles that name was taken to be my real one and the manager would call me Richard during consultative and safety meetings a few years later. Those sitting at the table who knew different just smirked.

Boring the holes in the right place and right depth, with little or no room to work on the face side of the moving armoured conveyor, took some mastering. We also needed to stem up the holes with the right amount of powder and the right delayed detonators in sequence.

The explosives were picked up pre-shift on the surface from a small building in the pit yard half buried in the ground and made of concrete. On each stick, or pill, was the name PENOBEL. The Nobel Prize is named after the inventor of dynamite. Alfred Nobel also owned an armaments company and was known as "the Merchant of Death" before bequeathing his wealth to set up the Nobel Prize system.

The drilled holes were then filled with a non-explosive stemming, and long plastic tubes of water or sometimes gel to stop them just blowing back. Not damaging the thin wires was important.

A white cable was passed over the face conveyor and the orange detonator wires connected to make a circuit. One miner went up the face on sentry duty to prevent anyone getting near the impending explosion and then everyone else cleared off down the gate. The shot firer connected up to his battery, tested the circuit then shouted "FIRE".

If we had done the job right the coal was in heaps like black breakfast cereal. Big lumps were a sign that one or two of the holes had blown back out and interrupted the sequence. Big lumps made shovelling much harder. This area, once cleared of coal and supported, would allow a face machine to turn around its cutting disc and travel back taking another cut along the face to the tailgate end and then repeat the sequence.

There are simpler, more effective ways of mining coal, but this pit was slow to adapt and investment came through in a trickle. The problem was that three blokes blowing up coal and shovelling it onto the conveyor could not keep up with a modern coal-face machine. It was a high-pressure task on the face side and the lads were in a high-risk environment with so many ways to be maimed.

I've fond memories of the scrapes in the 'stable hole' and plenty of not so fond memories. But above all, I discovered I liked blowing stuff up for a living – it was in my blood.

○ ○ ○

As a trained faceworker it was important to be adaptable to whatever job you were deployed to, even if it was never part of your training. The installation and salvage of faces was a massive and complex job that became more important in the era of retreat faces. Many advanced faces were never salvaged and the kit left in situ. With pre-driven roadways and largely predictable geology, faces were worked out quicker and replacements needed to be kitted out in as short a time possible.

For a period, my team would be re-deployed to either salvaging a face that had been worked out, or installing a new face. This sometimes meant using new equipment or just moving the equipment from one face to another. The hydraulic supports needed moving – perhaps two hundred in some cases. They weighed tonnes. The armoured flexible conveyor needed to be installed. This would be up to 250 metres long in the pit I worked. So did the power units and the hydraulic pumps. Usually, last of all, the coal-face machines.

Most of this very heavy equipment was dragged by rope haulage machines and manhandled with smaller scale lifting gear. Some pits had specialist teams to carry out these tasks, but at my pit, coal-cutting teams were drafted in to get the replacement face up and running. Pit work was often about adaptability and improvisation – how to make do in very difficult and tight circumstances with minimum mechanical assistance. As face equipment got bigger, the equipping and salvaging of faces became more difficult and therefore even more important to prevent production gaps.

Over the years I worked down the pit, much of the work changed through technological advances, but the routine was essentially the same. There was always a relentless drive to keep the coal flowing. Plenty of machinery, but still the same old problems that had to be solved by the brains and brawn of coal miners. Coal mining, I realised, was about the basics – keeping the roof away from the floor and maintaining ventilation. If you can't do that, you can't mine coal. I was no longer a rookie; the coal face became a way of life for me, but working shifts and gobbling dust had its drawbacks.

The Government promotional films of the era, with no hint of irony, declared:

The people of Britain are building
Drilling out from their native rock
The foundations of the future

To coal we must now turn again
For all the strength that we shall need
In the years to come[24]

During the hectic period as a newly trained face worker, I became a dad for the first time, so everything was new – not just the lack of sleep. My little girl, Kate, was born in Northern General Hospital in Sheffield – a tiny baby who emerged into the world without a murmur. The midwife hung her up from her ankles and whacked her on the soles of her feet. The little 'un burst into life and screamed her head off – thereby clearing her lungs of any unhelpful fluid.

It is bewildering to look back and think about so much happening – so much to take in and so much to do. It was non-stop and frantic – where did anyone find the time? How did the time go so quickly?

Kids; buying houses; earning money but not enough; responsibilities; worries; getting older. What happened to the revolution? It looks like it will have to wait – I'm on night shift this week.

One minute the children are in nappies, then off to school. Before long they are doing A levels. Then having jobs, their own home and relationships and having kids themselves. What happened there? Blink and you've missed it.

---

24 J Willgoose Esq, Public Service Broadcasting, *Every Valley, The Pit*, 2017.

Choggers. Acrylic on canvas. © David J Parry.

3

THROUGH THE GLASS – 'THE PAST WE INHERIT.'[25]

Rolling countryside with woodland, shallow vales and farmland surrounded the villages in the area. Green swathes of colour in the spring, golden in late summer and furrowed brown in the last few months of the year. There was plenty of wildlife if you knew what to look for. Birds chirped in the trees and soared on the wing. Lapwings thrived in the scrubby grassland around the industrial waste along with skylarks soaring vertically and noisily into blue skies and puffy white clouds. Wildfowl made their own tumultuous racket in the flashes – numerous shallow flooded areas, caused by subsidence.

   This mix of countryside, wildlife and industry was typical of coal mining areas. Miners, unlike working people in the big towns and cities, were often very rural in their ways of life and their forefathers would probably have worked on the land not that long ago. Foraging in the woods and keeping animals for the pot were common practices and maintained old ties to country ways.

   Dark mounds were dotted around, well proud of the expected horizon,

---

25 National Union of Mineworkers motto: *'The past we inherit, the future we build.'*

and some were adorned with mechanical devices reminiscent of fairground rides. The sound of clattering steel could be picked up if the wind was in the right direction. At times, when the weather was dry, clouds of dark dust would swirl around these odd peaks and huge mounds. To the north the coking plant belted out its smoky contribution to the scene. Then a huge plume of white steam climbed into the sky like a mini atom bomb as the white-hot coke was quenched with water. The smell of chlorine could often be caught on the wind. Further down the broad shallow valley another coke works gave forth its own tower of swirling steam.

Unseen from a distance was the old canal winding its way between the two villages – its presence betrayed only for a few hundred yards by a high embankment and strips of hawthorn bushes. The canal once connected the river Calder navigation near Wakefield with the South Yorkshire navigation east of Rotherham. It was no longer a working waterway and the coal barges were long since gone. One or two were sunk in the shallow water. The towpath provided one of the many country walks in the area and an adventure playground for carefree kids like myself.

Difficult to spot at first was the railway, but every train and locomotive that passed could be seen from the main road easily enough, gliding through the open land. Yet more smoke and steam, yet more wagons of coal on their way across the country, this way and that. Hidden from view were the engine sheds, locomotives lined up abreast in front of them. All had pretty much the same black and dirty appearance. Ashes from the firebox smouldered alongside them, filling the air with a pungent aroma.

The main line was part of the LMS (London, Midland and Scottish Railway.) Express trains, from Scotland to London or cross country to the south west, passed this way with locomotives – some of them in dark green livery – high on the train spotter's list. They thundered through, beguiling to me and to most young lads, who rarely travelled outside the locality.

Uncle Richard was a quiet, dignified man. At least, that is how he always appeared each Sunday morning in the late 1950s as we three kids, taken by our dad, knocked on his door. We walked each Sunday to the nearby cemetery to pay respects to Grandmother. In truth, none of us kids really remembered her but Dad's weekly trip meant everything to him. He did not seem capable of sharing grief or seeking help from those close to him. Nothing was ever said about his sense of loss. Brought up with no father of his own from an early age, he never got over her death and clung to her memory until he too shared the same cemetery.

A few quiet moments with some empty stares – she had no headstone – and it was on to uncle's little house about ten minutes' walk away. As we entered, Uncle was sitting at the kitchen table with a large breakfast of thick ham and eggs with bright yellow yolks and some white sliced bread. This kind of breakfast was unfamiliar to my brother, sister and me; Weetabix was about as good as it got for us.

He had a big mug of tea, which he sipped quietly. We sat and behaved ourselves and only spoke when spoken to. My older brother and I had matching blazers, short trousers and leather sandals. Mam had made most of our clothes herself.

Manners were important to the family. Any kind of uncouth behaviour was a breach of the family code. Richard always seemed particularly reserved and well-mannered and it was a bit of a puzzle how he functioned with scores of coal miners to supervise. But that is what he did for a living.

A big radio in a shining wooden cabinet was turned on, providing background noise from the BBC Light Programme. The radio had a huge dial with names on it from around the world. This impressed my younger self no end – a machine in contact with the rest of the world! And all places I would remember as I progressed through school, geography lesson after geography lesson.

There wasn't much chit-chat at the family gathering – neither Uncle Richard nor Dad were big on small talk. Some talk of weather and then maybe some pit talk. This was a language I was fascinated by but I could not make head or tail of it. Words and phrases with no connection to any reality I knew were exchanged between the two men with casual ease: 'Main gate, tail gate, cross gate, inbye, outbye, paddy, rip, gob,' – the mind boggled. Many years later I too shared the same mysterious language of the pitmen.

The fire in the jet-black range spat and Dad gave it a poke and half a bucket of additional coal, knowing the gathering was about to come to an end.

"Well … time I was off down the club" said Richard turning off the radio and putting on his sports jacket. His accent was Yorkshire but not broad. He was a big man, about six foot – same as Dad, but a little stockier. Clean-shaven and well-groomed, he strode towards the back door and placed a trilby on his head covering his thinning Brylcreemed hair. My dad plonked his flat cap back on and, one by one, we all left the house. Locking the door, Richard commented again on the weather, casting a glance to the west. We walked together up the short street to the lane.

Noisy dogs and laughter greeted us. On Sunday mornings young men with little snapping terriers were a common sight. They crossed the lane into a field next to the pit tip with a firearm. Young men with guns were not particular about what they shot.

My family group strolled together up through the village past the chapel with the grey pit tip glowering high over the sports field. A flock of racing pigeons, white and grey feathers standing out from the dark background of the looming spoil heap, swooped in formation.

I was to return to the same chapel many years later for the funeral of my father.

Richard took an abrupt left and before entering the club said his good-byes. It was another mile or so back to the village where we now lived and we kids dug in for the effort and wondered what Uncle Richard was doing in a club full of blokes drinking beer. I'm sure he drank in moderation.

Our family of five had started life together in that same little house along with Grandmother and Uncle Richard. We moved to a terrace house in the next village when I was three years old. My mother had three kids in quick succession. This was perhaps not unusual for the time but nevertheless, a daunting task for any mother.

I can't remember too much about living with Grandma and Uncle Richard but seven people in such a small dwelling must have been very difficult. It speaks volumes for Grandma that she was happy to put up with it. Grandma died and Richard was left there alone. He had not yet married and did not do so until he was in his fifties. Unusual for the 1950s, he spent his holidays abroad in exotic locations sending postcards from places I had to look up in the atlas.

Uncle Richard was a colliery official and the last of the family to actually help run a coal mine rather than just work in it. His father was an under-manager in the same pit and he in turn was the son of the pit manager. All men in the family played some role in managing the local collieries. Richard's own uncle had taken his mining expertise to France in the Great War and spent his time tunnelling under enemy trenches and blowing them up. He stayed in France until the early 1920s, dealing with the war legacy: unexploded ordinance. Blowing stuff up ran in the family.

The house that Richard lived in was built by his grandfather. In fact, many of the houses in the village were built by the same man; he had come over from North Wales in about 1880 to run the colliery. Mostyn Quay Colliery on the Flintshire Coast in North Wales was victim to a catastrophic flood that left the entire workforce without a job, including the manager – Richard's grandfather. With a testimonial from William Gladstone's son Stephen, a rector in Flintshire, he was appointed manager of a new colliery just north of Barnsley. Many members of his workforce followed, some pushing handcarts containing their belongings all the way from North Wales.

And so, my great grandfather was the founding father of a Welsh community in the South Yorkshire village. The family were held in high esteem, having provided jobs and houses for incoming Welsh people and others seeking employment in the expanding Yorkshire coalfield. However, the economic pressures on the community in the twenties and thirties took their toll. War, followed by unemployment, destitution for some and a hard grind to get through the days, months and years, took the shine off any former standing in the community for the family.

The 1926 strike and subsequent depression hit coal mining areas hard and even those with jobs struggled. The miners were on strike for months; the General Strike only lasted a week. There was more of this sacrifice to come decades later.

A family, comfortably off by local standards, started to feel the pinch. Grandmother lost two husbands. With no breadwinner, she battled on and my dad knew only too well the resilience and hard work required to bring up four kids. She was on the local council and worked tirelessly for the Red Cross. Dad's weekly walks to the cemetery are testament to his devotion.

The only extended family member well known to the public was 'Our Chuck's son', as Dad usually called him. William, my great grandad's youngest son, married Jane Elizabeth Taylor. Their son was Tommy Taylor who worked at the pit for a short time before becoming a footballer with Barnsley, Manchester United and England. He was killed in the Munich air disaster of 1958 along with many others of the famous Manchester United 'Busby Babes' team.

As a young kid, I stood with my mother in the village of Monk Bretton, the crowds were a revelation. It was Tommy Taylor's funeral. Mother's younger brother, Jack, also played football for Barnsley at that time and Mam knew Tommy from when he was a little kid. The grave was a miniature floral football pitch with a huge ball of flowers on the centre spot.

An accident – shattered lifeless bodies followed by funerals – became a theme in my young mind. Some years later I was to learn that six of the players in the Manchester United squad came from coalmining backgrounds and that Matt Busby and his assistant, Jimmy Murphy were both ex-miners. Not unusual it seems – Bill Shankly, Liverpool's famous manager, was an Ayrshire collier.

My father remained a collier all his working life. But then, Richard did not quite make the grade of the previous generation either. He had done all the training and all the mining exams but remained an official who worked, in his later career, for most part in the surveyors' office. He was more than likely not pushy enough to order men around. Managing colliers is not much fun if they ignore you.

Richard was comfortable with anonymity. As a young mine official in 1936 events took over.

Great Grand-parents. Acrylic on canvas. © David J Parry.

4

"HEARTS THAT LOVED NEVER FORGET."[26]

Some bloke must have dragged his sorry backside down the pit lane to start his shift for the last time, but he never had the chance to repeat the humdrum routine. Leaving the noise and back-chat in the family house, that bloke joins a stream of other blokes near the pit, shuffling along with little enthusiasm for the coming shift. Day-dreaming about better things, better days. But now on a date with destiny.

The little rituals and hopes for a better future erased. Lost forever as the night shift became perpetual night for that bloke and all blokes like him. Someone, somewhere is paying the price.

Taking a detour to the pub and not turning up for work has its downsides. Perhaps the sack. Maybe just a bollocking from management and a black mark in his attendance record. For some though, it's the start of the rest of their lives. That one bit of good luck stacked up against all the bad. If you don't turn up you can't get injured or blown up.

---

26 South Yorkshire Times, 13 August 1936.

"Bye love – see you in the morning. I expect you'll be up. Tuck the kids in tight."

But what if *you* are the one that dies? A terrifying moment when you realise, then shock and hopefully not too much pain. You will not know and you may not care, but this shift is the one that puts you in the history books. You die – they all die in an instant. It's the most common way working people make history. Dying together, in ways that few can understand, proves an irresistible magnet to news media and the curious bystander alike.

Making history isn't so easy – there has to be pain and sacrifice. Joy always comes way down the list for what makes news and what makes history. The battlefield, the flood, the fire – count the dead, line them up.

One early morning of August 6th 1936 an explosion ripped through Wharncliffe Woodmoor colliery[27] and 58 lives were snuffed out. None of my father's family were working in those early hours. Rescue teams did what they could but the one survivor later died of his injuries. Five canaries expired in the post-explosion gases.

Death and injury were common in the coal mining industry but this disaster was national news.

> 'The explosion appears to have been one of great violence, and was followed by falls of roof and a rush of air and gas … '[28]

The King, Edward VIII, sent a message of sympathy and a relief fund was quickly set up with the singer and film star Gracie Fields, amongst many others, donating £100 – a tidy sum in 1936.

The Labour plan for 'socialisation' of the coal industry was brought forward and published the day after the disaster, with Walter Citrine commenting on the perils of coal mining.[29]

The HM Medical Inspector of Mines, Sydney Fisher, concluded later that, in 'all but two cases, carbon monoxide poisoning was the cause of death'.

---

27 There were two pits in the village of Carlton – Wharncliffe Woodmoor, known as Old Carlton and Carlton Main, known as New Carlton.
28 Colliery Guardian, 7 August 1936.
29 General Secretary of the Trades Union Congress, 1926–1946.

Many of the horrific injuries occurred *after* death in subsequent explosions and falls of ground.[30]

However, in the aftermath, it was my uncle's job to carry out a site observation of the underground scene. This practice is an essential part of all reporting of accidents in coal mines under the various rules of the Mines & Quarries Acts. A written account of what can be observed as soon as possible after the event is required. The idea is for the observer to dispassionately describe the site and resist the temptation to interpret what is seen, leaving that to others.

Uncle's account in note form on this lay in an envelope for 70 years until I stumbled upon them. Unsure if it was a dark secret or not, I wondered about their provenance.

After my dad died in 2000, my brother and I had the job of clearing up years and years of paper work, bric-a-brac, old clothes, and dumping what seemed worthless. There was, in truth, not much care taken; one man's history left in a skip.

Years later I found a small tatty envelope containing even tattier leaves of paper ripped from a notebook. They were pencil written and smeared with dirt. These were observation notes and two memos from management in the same envelope but they did not add up. I knew what I had found was a report from underground in a colliery. After all, I was to write many such scruffy notes myself as part of my safety role for the NUM branch in the 1980s and 1990s. I did not, and still don't know, the significance of the notes from management.

These notes were not easily readable by anyone other than the person who wrote them. Still, they convey in a chilling matter-of-fact way the scene underground after the explosion.

7th August 1936

No 9 Face
At the cc m/c [coal cutting machine]) probably 30 yds from low end of the

---

[30] Colliery Guardian, 15 August 1936.

cc m/c found cable in and apparently cutting. 1 man behind m/c pointing towards 9s level, left leg over pans – on back.

Two men jammed in between the cc m/c and conveyor, one on top of another – the head of one was battered in and blood on the pans with both lying on stomach and heads uphill. Covered with timber which appeared to have been blown out from below. No face supports below m/c so far as could see 10 yds supports blown out about 30 yds above the conveyor from next to m/c with face side higher than gob side and some gob timber shows signs of weight.

1st oil lamp No 346 facing inbye. L/4 Oldham on back, head facing outbye. No 89 Aldwarke[31] on stomach facing outbye.

Approx 30 yds above is the body of a m/c man apparently was there attending with driver, the body was on side with head in face and feet against the pans in a v-shape. V points uphill, small of back against prop, 8 inches from face – arm against rear.

Body A about 25 yds farther up the face. Oil lamp Deputy type, No 16 standing on the bottom next face, apparently undamaged.

100 yds outbye from face on Top Gate, body B lying on back, head pointing towards face and outbye. Lamp 400 Aldwarke Electric No64 [name] 1 yd outbye of him.

Body C
295 yds outbye (approx) of face, No 9 Top Gate lying on face and looking outbye in huddled up position. Aldwarke Lamp No 100 lying on its side against his left elbow. Clothes by his side.

Body D
305 yds from face (Top Gate. Face downwards and head facing in inbye, clutching shirt with Rt hand, stick against Rt side, no lamp (L Boyd).

---

31 Types of miners' lamps.

Body E
312 yds from face No 9 Top Gate lying back head facing outbye left arm across chest. No lamp (Wilson chocker).

Body F
2 yds from E face down pointing inbye Aldwarke Lamp No 88 lying under arm at his side Rt. Hands crossed.

Body G
Lying 6 yds from F – lying on right arm under head and head outbye. Aldwarke No 89 lamp by left hand. A White – ripper.

Body H
8 yds from G outbye lying on back head outbye. Aldwarke No 74 lamp on neck strap (Deputy – Sawyer.)

Body I
Removed. A Hinchcliffe – got particulars.

No one had any idea that in the early hours such a tragedy could unfold. Yet kept in the same envelope as the site observation notes were two signed memos from management to my uncle.

30 June 1936 –
I want results of air samples taken at Nos 4 & 5 pits sent to my office in addition to those taken at 1, 2 & 3.

4th August 1936
Re: your reports of yesterday:-
Blacketts Return end 0.7% CH4
No 1s Low gate 0.3%

These figures do not reconcile each other. Blacketts return air is intake air on 1s Low gate + one would naturally expect that the %age of gas would if anything be higher on 1s Low gate. Try these points again at the earliest opportunity.[32]

> 5≠ 9' Face
> Body D. 305 yds from face
> 9' Topgate. Face downwards
> Totd facing inbye, clutching shirt
> with rt hand. stick against
> rt side. No Lamp (L Boyd)
>
> Body E. 312 yds from face
> No 9' Top gate, lying back
> half facing outbye, left arm
> across chest. NO Lamp
> (Wtbox Chocked)
>
> Body F 2 yds from E. Face
> down pointg inbye
> aldwinkle lamp No 88 lying
> at his side rt) unfastened Hands
> crossed.

A page from the 1936 Site Observers Notes.

---

32 Original notes can now be found in Barnsley Archives.

Perhaps only my uncle knew the significance of these notes – but then again, only in hindsight. Two days later the fatal combination of methane and an ignition occurred. It was left to the living to try to fathom out why.

The Inquiry eventually pointed to, but did not conclude, that there were three key aspects resulting in the disaster:

- Air doors had been 'spragged' open[33] and this led to a short circuit of the ventilation system inviting a build-up of gas. (Presumably haulage workers were trying to make their job easier.)

- Although holes had been drilled for shotfiring, the shots had not been fired – suggesting the shot firer had picked up a high gas reading on his lamp.

- A commutator on the inbye loader motor was found on the floor and the cover was loose (an electrician had been deployed to overhaul electrical equipment).

This last piece of evidence endured as the source of the explosion and seems very plausible. Electrical equipment was not designed in those days to be 'intrinsically safe' for underground working.

Explosions resulting from electrical equipment continued to beset the British coal industry until recent times. At Houghton Main (near Barnsley) five men lost their lives when a ventilation fan ignited methane in 1975. In Lancashire, Goldborne Colliery was the scene of an underground explosion. Ten men lost their lives and one was seriously injured on 18 March 1979. An auxiliary ventilation fan was also to blame. There were 40 casualties with severe burns at the North Lanarkshire, Cardowan Colliery in 1982 – another 'firedamp' (methane) explosion.

In addition to the investigation into the source of ignition in 1936, it was thought that a lack of recent stone dusting had contributed to the spread

---

33 Air doors should be closed before another set are opened. Wooden props or similar could have been used to keep one or more set of doors open.

of the explosion. Stone dust (limestone) is used underground to reduce the risk of coal dust igniting. Stone dust can suffocate fires and 'dilutes' the amount of coal dust around. Uncle Richard had given evidence to the Inquiry on dust sampling on the district and they proved to be at normal levels. Nevertheless, much of the stone dust was damp and therefore much less effective at suffocating explosive flames.

Richard was in no way implicated in any failure of duty. Key questions remained, but clearly certain practices needed looking at and revising. Regardless of this lack of certainty about why it happened, the brutal fact was that methane and an electrical spark did combine to blow up that part of the mine and 58 men lost their lives. The ineffectiveness of stone dust to limit the range of the explosion was a lesson learnt, as was more vigilance when overhauling electrical equipment.

The history of coalmining is that of lessons being learnt, but often too slowly. A colliery only two miles away, North Gawber, with the same owners, had lost 19 miners killed in an explosion less than a year earlier. The Inquiry followed a similar path with many of the same questions asked but its findings were unable to prevent the subsequent explosion and greater loss of life.

As for me, the notes about unusual gas readings from management to my uncle throw up more questions than answers. Something was amiss but a problem with ventilation was only hinted at. The notes were in the same envelope as the site observation report kept for decades and are clearly linked. The gas readings were not high but could not be 'reconciled' with the ventilation system. Anybody who might know more is long since dead.

That mysterious pit talk I heard in childhood was to become part of my daily life. This mining disaster was all too real and all too near, despite the yawning gap in time. The background anxiety about injury and death stalked me, sometimes just a little and sometimes much more. It was back with each word I read of the notes. A rising anxiety and lump in the throat. As a kid I was unable to throw off this shadow as neighbours were killed and injured. Dad left the house every working day and always without fail a little nagging fear crept up on me, if only for a split second – would he come home in one piece?

Many years later, in 2018, my partner was recording the experiences of a retired miner from the Dearne Valley. He told the story of his wife's family and about a fatality underground in the 1920s. The miner was killed by a fall of ground, but on his death certificate this was attributed to 'An act of God.' So many acts of God. Who else can you blame? Certainly not the mining company.

These 'acts of God' were, it seems, particularly common in coal mining. In 1838 at Huskar pit, Silkstone, near Barnsley twenty-six children drowned in a flooded coal mine. This too was attributed to the Almighty.

Sitting in a Barnsley library turning the pages of the official Inquiry into the disaster I stared at the date again: 1936. Many hundreds of miles south of this scene of death and destruction other miners, some of them from Barnsley, were facing yet more death and destruction – volunteers in the International Brigades. The Spanish Civil War was also taking its toll and making a much bigger mark in history.

One such volunteer was an associate of my father. Tommy Degnan was the stuff of legend. A Wigan miner, he volunteered in the First World War only to be taken prisoner and end up working coal as forced labour in Poland. After the war he moved to Barnsley to find a job back in the pit. His activism resulted in him being sacked and he worked tirelessly in the unemployed movement of the time and took part in the hunger marches. He got a job again at Wharncliffe Woodmoor in the early 1930s. When the Civil War in Spain broke out, he joined the International Brigades with other British miners. He swapped the dangers of explosions underground for the bombs, bullets and shells of battle. He was in Spain when the pit blew up. A little later he returned to Barnsley after being wounded by one of Franco's mortar shells.

Tommy became an NUM Branch Official at my father's pit. Dad knew Tommy, but rarely spoke of this association to his kids. Nevertheless, tales of fighting Oswald Mosley's Black Shirts in Barnsley filtered through from time to time.

Tommy was the archetypal Communist Party agitator and was to mentor a young miner in the fifties and sixties – Arthur Scargill.

So called 'acts of God', 'industrial accidents', and disasters of most kinds were to be logged in my psyche, especially when they were clearly avoidable. Health and safety matters had become ingrained in me. I could not avoid re-running my safety training every time such an event appeared in the newspapers or on television. There was a hidden trigger that started my brain looking for sequences of actions and events.

One such instance was the Grenfell Tower fire disaster in 2017 and the subsequent inquiry. I was in London at the time and was re-directed onto a different Tube line to avoid the fire. At the subsequent inquiry an executive at one of the companies supplying the dangerous inflammable cladding was forced to admit he told building companies questioning the safety of the product to "go fuck themselves". He also remarked that such people were "mistaking" (him) "for someone who gives a damn!"[34] And there you have it: some people *don't* give a damn about anything other than profit. The inquiry lumbered on for years afterwards and the grieving are left to grieve.

Some people may ask each other, 'What were you doing in the Cuban missile crisis? When Jack Kennedy was shot? When the Twin Towers fell?' I ask myself, 'Where was I when Grenfell was ablaze or when the pit tip slid into the school in Aberfan?'

On the face of it there is no comparison with pit disasters. Yet it was immediately clear, decades of hard lessons learnt about buildings, tower blocks and fires had been conveniently forgotten. Standards were falling and society was going backwards. Health and Safety had become a burden. Profit came first – the loss was in lives.

Oh let's not think about tomorrow, lest we disappointed be
Our joys may turn to sorrow as we may daily see[35]

---

34 *Guardian* newspaper, 30 November 2020.
35 *The Trimdon Grange Explosion*, Tommy Armstrong (1890s).

Wharncliffe Woodmoor Disaster 1936. Acrylic on canvas. © David J Parry.

5

EARLY DAYS – GROWING UP AND GETTING OUT

As a lad, when I peered out of the bedroom window, I could see three pits. The 'family' pit was not in view, nestling as it was behind a rise in the south west. The main colliery next to Royston, my village, was New Monckton. Its six shafts dominated the landscape with its big winding tower, coal preparation plant, coke ovens and spoil heaps. Marshalling yards covered acres of land next to the main railway line and a ten-foot-high notice told rail passengers the National Coal Board were busy mining precious coal for the nation. The 1950s were the years when the country cried out for more and more coal.

Pits there were in abundance and along with them working men's clubs. In the village I grew up in there were no less than seven clubs. Two were part of the Miners' Welfare Scheme and two were tied to the railways and big loco sheds. The others were independent. In addition, there were four pubs. Every pub and club had their sports teams.

There were two infant schools, one of which was Church of England, and a junior school. A secondary modern school was spread over a swathe of land in the middle of the village. The grammar schools were in the towns of Barnsley, Wakefield and Normanton.

An 11th century Norman church stood proud over the village dwellings. It was considered 'high church', I was told by people who know about such matters. I attended carol services there with junior school and read from a huge wood-carved lectern the stories of Jesus, Mary and Joseph. There was no room in the inn, I informed the congregation. These people were treated like outsiders in their own country. Modern-day Palestinians know what that feels like. Herod and Pontius Pilate had their part to play, but infanticide and Roman imperialism were merely context to the main tale of a virgin birth and later developments involving executions on the cross. The smell of incense and polished wood in the church infused my memories.

There were also plenty of chapels to keep the Wesleyans, Baptists, Salvation Army and others happy. We kids briefly attended the Sally Army. They had a good brass band to march around with and, at the time, it seemed a bit more interesting than the solemnity of the church or chapel.

Our house was half-way up a long street of terraces. There were eight houses for every common backyard with an entry to access the yards. Shared toilets were in a short row with a place for the dustbins and each dwelling had its own coal house. Old Uncle Ernie, from next door, spent a fair amount of time in the toilet so timing was everything when you needed to pay a visit.

The Home Coal lorry from the nearby pit would drop off a ton of concessionary coal in the yard. A miner was allowed nine tons per year at the time. From a relatively early age, my brother and I would shovel the coal into the coal house. It involved placing planks of wood across the doorway, filling a few shovels, then putting another plank across of in succession until the little building was pretty much full.

Behind the house was an area of open ground they called 'The Square'. Other terrace rows were beyond and orchards with apples and pears. Around this open land were pigeon lofts and hen huts. Before off-track betting was legalised, there was also an old railway truck used as a betting shop. It was busy on Saturdays with look-outs posted to keep an eye out for the police.

As a kid this way of life seemed timeless, rooted in some ancient decree that pits and pit villages would last beyond any known horizon. I did not know any different. There was no television in our house and views and images of any other world were rare and fleeting.

Yet it wasn't just growing up and moving on that changed everything for me; all that seemed solid and predictable was soon to alter beyond recognition.

My life was to go in one direction and that of the communities I lived in another. Despite the divergence, the emotional ties and common history were intertwined for all time.

I had first been aware of the effects of pit closures in the early sixties. Dad had been moved twice as pits shut. I remembered the furore in 1966 when they announced the closure of the local pit, Monckton Main. It had received huge investment in the 1950s and stood as a monument to nationalisation. The 'secure future in coal' boasted by so many Coal Board promotion films was in clear evidence to the nation. Yet the confidence of the early years of nationalisation soon faded. Pits in Durham, Scotland and Wales took the brunt of the closures of the 1960s.

I was very much at ease with the industrial and rural setting of a pit village. The fields, railways and canals provided an endless source of adventure for a lad with a gang of mates. Traffic and crossing the road were hazards yet unheard of. But as childhood blended into the teenage years, tensions and unease increased. Being brought up in a pit village had its drawbacks and consequences that were difficult to track. Restlessness, conflicts and confrontations became more common. The cause and effect were not very clear but those tensions were to provide a constant sub-plot to the rest of my life.

For instance, when I first got a job in the coal industry early in 1977, I was naturally enough unfamiliar with pit work. In fact, I had little interest thus far in working down the pit. My parents had even less interest in their kids working in the coal industry. But, having taken the plunge in my mid-twenties, I would be quickly trained up and become very familiar with pit work. There is nothing innate to being a miner – no one is born to it. But the connections and history seemed inescapable and grew in me regardless, influencing the choices I was to make.

Mining had attractions for me, but pit villages did not. The set up was too claustrophobic and tribal. The pit village I came to work in many years later was smaller but very much like the one I had been brought up in. It suited me to keep a wary distance.

My background was largely unknown to the fellow miners I was to work with. I was considered something of an outsider at the pit where I ended up working; no one knew me or my past.

I had initially tried to get a job at Houghton Main colliery near Barnsley. The journey from north Sheffield was doable on shifts. I was put on some kind of waiting list. Not being convinced that this route was taking me anywhere, I called in at the NCB recruitment office in Barnsley. The best bet, I was advised, was to call in at my father's pit, South Kirkby. The traditional route into mining was via family connections. This was not an attractive option – South Kirkby was a long drive from Sheffield and anyway, I wanted to stay clear of my dad who had not yet retired.

A little later I responded to a recruitment advert by the NCB at a local labour exchange in Sheffield. The 'Plan for Coal' was underway with new investment in some of the older pits and also the opening of the Selby coalfield in North Yorkshire. Many older miners had taken early voluntary retirement and new labour was needed to restore manpower levels.

I recall being classed as 'green labour' [36] when I first got the job at Thurcroft with a number of other lads travelling in from Sheffield. This grated with me because my family had been working in the coal industry decades before this pit had even been sunk. Having a mining pedigree seemed to matter to me – a curious form of pride.

The shafts at this pit were sunk by Irish labourers along with their itinerant families. Everybody was an incomer to the new villages springing up next to the pits of the expanding Yorkshire coalfield. I was to work with Scots, Geordies, Cumbrians and Welsh – most of whom had settled in the village. The other incomers were from Rotherham area pits that had closed and the recruited men from around Sheffield.

My commitment to the union and work mates was never in question.

---

36 'Green labour' was anyone thought to be not from mining stock.

Yet when I briefly considered living once again in a pit village, my kinship ties elsewhere soon put the thought from my mind. That desire for distance from the day-to-day life of the pit village – any pit village – remained.

That estrangement from pit village life can be explained, in part, by one simple thing that had so many consequences. I passed my 11+ exam and then went to grammar school. A very short chapter in my life, but arguably the most significant. From that day in 1962 I was never one of them. No matter what undercurrents of pride and attachments survived the following decades – I was an outsider.

In the beginning, passing this seemingly innocuous exam put unseen pressure on my relationship with my two siblings. They left school and went to work. My brother did an engineering apprenticeship but when he was married with kids he went down the pit to earn more money. My sister worked in shops in Barnsley and then in sewing factories along with my mother. For me it was 'A' levels and university. 'Golden bollocks' went on to gain a modest degree but at some cost to myself and to relationships with the people and places where I was brought up.

I was required to wear a school uniform and walk to the railway station near the pit to get the train to school – a peculiar West Riding County Council arrangement. Returning from school I had to put up with the local kids from the pit rows in the east of the village. A school uniform was a sure sign of someone worth baiting, someone worth a kicking.

I spent time with grammar school pupils and young people from my village – two often very different worlds. My accent stood out at school but I was thought to talk a bit different around the pit village. This village was a curious mix of South Yorkshire with a little bit of Staffordshire – only a faint difference but with some different names for everyday things. It wasn't a Barnsley accent – that was often incomprehensible to outsiders. I could manage to pass for a Barnsley lad everywhere except in Barnsley.

Welsh was still spoken by a few in the village of my birth until into the 1980s. Scottish miners and their kids in Yorkshire hung on to their accents for decades. The same was true, for example, of the Northampton steel town, Corby, where a Scottish accent is very common.

Occasionally, resentment – created in the main by the social divisions of the 11+ system – waylaid me. On the canal bank one summer day an adversary showed up with a 0.22 BSA air rifle. Various forms of weapons were popular with young males. There was the usual exchange of verbal abuse but the lad on the other bank decided he would take it further. He shot me in the thigh from across the canal. It may well not have been intentional (a bad shot perhaps?) but the sensation of the slug ripping into my leg was real enough.

It was a mile and half home. There was pain but hardly any blood. Mother was summoned from the shirt factory at the bottom of the street and I was taken to hospital and the pellet was removed. I remember seeing the X-ray with the little metal lump nestling against my thigh bone. No general anaesthetic; I was given just gas, like in the dentists of the time. I was not quite unconscious and sensed the incision and search for the foreign body. In a daze and feeling nauseous I was taken home. I recalled the removal of my tonsils a couple of years previously and was beginning to develop a bit of a phobia about hospitals.

My mother reported the lad to the police. To this day I have no idea what, if any, action was taken. The offender and I came across each other again on a number of occasions but never spoke. I knew I was the outsider, the misfit. At the first opportunity I determined I wasn't going to hang around if I could help it.

Common among lads, I believe, my teenage years witnessed a long drawn-out, low-level conflict with my father. We did not see eye-to-eye. The best idea was to keep quiet and tip toe around him. This was made easier because he worked shifts. But on the odd occasion there were angry exchanges. This was put down to a clash of Welsh tempers. On reflection, I was to come to the conclusion that I was a bit of a pillock as a teenager.

My brother and sister followed a very different path. They went out to work for a living whilst I continued to attend school. I had newspaper rounds to try to earn a bit of cash for myself – pocket money was not on offer. Getting home earlier than the rest of his working family, I would do house chores and often cooked a meal for everyone. Vesta Chow Mein was popular with my siblings but certainly not my father who had very conservative tastes. Dad hardly ever cooked but when he did it was a masterpiece – chips and egg.

Eventually, I found an exit door to my early life in a pit village: higher education. Once I left for university in 1969, I only went back to my parents to work between term times. This was either on the Christmas post, or at a local carpet factory on twelve-hour night shifts in the summer holidays. I worked on a huge machine putting the latex/rubber backing to carpets. Not much skill involved and after a few days not very engaging. It was at the end of the sixties and many ex-miners worked there because it was better paid. I remember one spell when a very heavy-duty carpet came off the machine shift after shift. It was on order for the QE2 liner.

With my own earned money and the now obsolete state grant, I was largely financially independent. Student debt at that time was minimal.

Competent at academic studies, especially history, I also had talent at art. The new University of Essex offered me a place with two Bs at A level to study History of Art. Neither my history or art teacher thought this was a sensible compromise, in fact the art teacher was incensed. But that is the path I took.

University was a revelation – a portal to another world. I mixed with posh women from Cheltenham Ladies College, and was a northern curiosity for the Home County set. But it seemed to add up to very little and came and went so quickly. Fumbling sex, and dodgy Yugoslavian wine were perhaps best forgotten. The music of those days, on the other hand, stood the test of time. The 1970 Bath Festival was a high point. We travelled in an old Morris van with 'Hot Rats'[37] daubed on the side and raised the National Liberation Front flag of the so-called Viet Cong. We did not just want peace in Vietnam; we wanted the communists to win. Led Zeppelin, Jefferson Airplane – you name it, many famous bands of the time took to the stage over the course of a very long day and night.

Then, at last, I met my first love. I managed to lose some of my edge and irritability – finally, it seems I was growing up. She was a 'lass' from Leeds and we both talked a similar northern language – a little uncomfortable with the BBC English of our fellow students. Her dad was from Sri Lanka

---

37 Frank Zappa Album.

(Ceylon, as it was known then). He came to the UK as a boy in 1928, enlisted in the Signals in 1941 and fought with the Eighth Army in North Africa. After the war, not surprisingly he got a job with the GPO which became British Telecomm. He married a Yorkshire 'lass' and they raised a family in Leeds. He was a staunch Catholic and pictures of him with his wife visiting the Pope had pride of place in their house.

We two young students shared radical politics, but I was now introduced to new understandings about feminism and issues of race and identity. There are lots of versions of 'us' and 'them'; class is just one form of oppression.

Academically I did not make the best use of my time and, much later, I realised that I was too young to seize the opportunities and potential of higher education. I had a degree before I was 21 years old and, at the time, it seemed of little consequence. For the next 24 years it was just a piece of paper in a desk.

Ask me about Renaissance masters – Giotto, Piero della Francesca, Albrecht Durer and I would have an informed opinion. On the German Expressionists I will have much to say – perhaps informative or maybe a bit too obscure. But then ask me about cutting a thousand metres of coal in a shift and I can be equally verbose. In fact, ask me about UK energy policy from 1947 to the present day and I am likely to bore you rigid. It's like trainspotting or Islay malt whisky – an acquired taste.

Miners' strikes were not new to me when 1984 kicked off. As a student I had been involved in the 1972 strike, putting up pickets in the student house and joining them in the early hours at wharves in East Anglia. *Street Fighting Man* by the Rolling Stones was the wake-up call in our little terrace house.[38]

I first met Arthur Scargill in the winter of 1972 at Essex University. A lecture theatre full of students and miners were lifted on his rhetoric. A group of students were invited to Grimethorpe during the strike and I went along. I was a bit apprehensive – lads from Royston had a habit of falling out with those from nearby Grimethorpe. Drinking in one of the pit clubs, we students were toasted like heroes in the candlelit rooms of the Three-Day-Week. The strike was biting and electricity was rationed.

---

38 According to Andy Beckett in *When the Lights Went Out* (2009), the "politically combustible" Essex University is the setting for *The History Man* – Malcolm Bradbury, 1975.

Finally, was this the revolution we had been looking for – like Paris in 1968? Students and workers taking on the bourgeoisie. No. Unfortunately just another young bloke's fantasy, a false dawn. The miners won the strike and bumped up their take-home pay, but nothing much really changed. For a young man wanting everything, the return to business as usual was nowhere near enough.

As a student of the late sixties and early seventies I attended protests and demonstrations regularly. The Vietnam War, Campaign for Nuclear Disarmament, Anti-Apartheid, Anti-Internment – you name it – I turned up to swell the numbers. 'Rent-a-mob' according to the Tory press. This was an accusation I railed against – the only people being paid were the police and journalists!

Broad issues and international struggles were one thing, but changing things nearer to home was another. I decided, with my partner, to be a bit more direct in support for people at the bottom of the pile and worked in the Claimants' Union movement. London 'lefties' led the way on this.

This led me to operating in Essex on local council estates. We were dealing with 'real people': single mothers, pensioners and disabled people, instead of privileged young students from the stockbroker belt. It was an eye opener, a different reality. Though it was not very different to the 'reality' I had escaped some years before to become a student.

There was some self-interest: students of the time could claim social security outside term time and getting to know the system was potentially a benefit to any adult not in full-time work. Occupying DHSS offices was a favourite tactic. It probably wasn't very effective, but it pulled in many claimants with endless tales of hassle trying to live from day-to-day.

In Essex this was short-lived and my partner and I moved back up north to Merseyside, attracted by the prospect of re-immersing ourselves amongst 'real' people and marching towards a better world. There was more than hint of misty-eyed romanticism about this decision, but a career was not on my to-do list.

There were lots of big ideas around at the time and it was easy to believe that real change was happening. A non-hierarchical, non-preachy, struggle-focused organisation called Big Flame seemed a good fit, so we both joined and worked with many good comrades for another ten years.

We supported the dockers and building workers in the strikes of 1972. This involved advice and practical help where possible to claim social security payments. In those days it was possible to claim social security for dependents in strikes and a bit of know-how about the benefits system helped strikers a lot. It was often back onto the streets, this time to try to defend building workers locked up – the Shrewsbury Pickets.

This political existence was mainly second hand. I always seemed to be on the outside supporting people on rent strike, leafleting the Ford Halewood factory on a weekly basis, selling leftie papers on the dock road, trying my hand leafleting the Turin FIAT factories. I even had the cheek to sell newspapers to striking miners at Bold and Sutton Manor pits in the St Helens area during the 1974 miners' strike.

One day it would be different – but not in my early twenties. Yet being a full-time, long-haired layabout was beginning to wear a bit thin.

I seemed to be on a mission, but a bit fuzzy about what the mission was. All the best motives seemed in place, but I had no driving ambition – no career prospects. I dabbled at teacher training but threw in the towel early on when asked to do teaching practice in a Jesuit school.

Something was burning a hole in me, something I could not run from. The past and the present was mixed into a volatile cocktail. Feelings go so deep, it's hard to dig them out. I could not really understand it. So, I left Liverpool for South Yorkshire to find something I had mislaid some years before. I still felt uncomfortable on the margins, claiming benefits and then getting a job driving. It all seemed so pointless.

An advert for *'A secure future in coal mining!'* could not be ignored. It's taking me back ... but to where?

Much later, looking back through a different lens, that 'secure future in mining' was definitely smoke and mirrors:

Continually experimenting with new ideas and techniques
Reconstructing
Developing
Modernising

I believe, I believe
In progress, in progress

Machines will do the heavy work
Men will supervise the machines
You owe much to these machines
Horsepower, not manpower
Brains not brawn

I believe in progress

I believe. I believe
In progress, in progress
I believe, I believe
In progress, in progress

These men look the same as they always looked
They talk as they have always talked
But before your eyes they are changing

I believe in progress

I believe. I believe
In progress, in progress
I believe, I believe
In progress, in progress

I believe in progress[39]

---

39 J. Willgoose Esq, Public Service Broadcasting, *Every Valley, Progress*. 2017. All material from *Every Valley* by kind permission of J. Willgoose Esq.

6

BLURRED VISIONS AND CONFLICT

The portents were not good. Margaret Thatcher had won the Falklands war in 1982 and fancied a further attempt to challenge the trades unions. She had started with the steel unions in 1980. Feeling her power consolidated, the National Union of Mineworkers came into her cross hairs. She must have remembered, even if few miners ever did, that Tory Prime Minister, Harold Macmillan had warned his colleagues in the 1950s: "Never take on the Brigade of Guards or the National Union of Mineworkers." Edward Heath, a later Tory Prime Minister, did not heed the advice and ended up in the political wilderness.

There was unfinished business for the Establishment. The Tories had made their plans in Opposition. In 1977, two years before Thatcher came to power, what became known as the Ridley Report[40] was first circulated to Tory strategists and leading politicians. *The Final Report of the Policy Group on the Nationalised Industries* outlined Tory plans for de-nationalisation and made

---

40 Nicholas Ridley MP Chaired the Nationalised Industry Policy Group.

specific plans to take on the miners but to go for a softer target such as steel first. Building up coal stocks at power stations, preparing a nationally mobile police force and seeking to fracture trade union solidarity were high on the to-do list.

A report in 1973 from Wilfred Miron, Chair of East Midlands Division to the Chair of the National Coal Board also contained long-term plans to take on the emerging left leadership of the NUM and re-engineer industrial relations. The introduction of the productivity, or bonus system, in 1978, was a key step to try and wrest back management control by weakening national unity. The 'productivity' system, eroded national solidarity and set miner against miner and pit against pit – as predicted by the left in the NUM.

Thatcher herself had stumbled into a confrontation well before the plans were in place. Pit closures were threatened just after the Falklands war and the NUM, led by pits under threat in South Wales, moved to act. A national ballot to oppose closures, other than for safety or exhaustion reasons, was conducted. The result was a big majority for industrial action in Yorkshire, Scotland and South Wales. Advised by people who had more long-term plans to knacker the unions, Thatcher backed down. But she was not going to leave it there.

The arrival of US 'hitman', Ian MacGregor, fresh from taking on the UK steel unions, signalled the gloves were well and truly off. He was on television visiting a pit in the North East. He was comically knocked over by the crowd assembled and seemed to take this dent to his pride personally.

Taking the democratic mandate from the ballot to oppose pit closures, an overtime ban was begun by the NUM in late 1983. After weeks of disciplined action, it was having an effect and coal production slowed dramatically.

The lads I worked with preferred cutting coal to sitting on their backsides. The faces we worked on usually delivered the goods. Our pit depended on them and their ability to overcome difficulties and keep up supplies to the big steelworks in Scunthorpe. Closure threats were far from anybody's mind. A national overtime ban seemed like the best way to put pressure on the NCB and still drag a wage every week. But it wasn't without its problems.

One afternoon shift my coaling team wandered inbye from the paddy train and found an overman along with the deputy manager working on the tail gate end setting supports to cover a fall of ground. Not a good idea at the best of times, but there was a national overtime ban and here were management doing work between shifts. At first, I didn't react and just paced up and down trying to think but I was quickly surrounded by my mates. Being a face representative on the NUM Branch Committee, they looked to me to lead.

"Either it's a fucking overtime ban or it's not."

"Well? What now?" They all chipped in.

Weighing up the situation, I decided it was no time to compromise or seek a quiet life. I could have tried to soft soap and calm things down and I did not really want to blow anything out of proportion, but the union position was clear enough.

"Not acceptable, Gaffer. You know the consequences," I said as I confronted the deputy manager next to the pack hole.

"Don't be hasty – we're we are only helping out. The face is now ready for coaling. Come on … " the deputy manager pleaded.

The overman knew me well and he also tried to calm things down.

Picking up the phone to the coal face in the other seam I informed them, "Deputy Manager and overman found doing NUM work in a national overtime ban. It's up to you but we are going home in protest."

A couple more calls to mates in the headings and the ball was rolling. Nothing else was needed. The news went round the pit in a matter of minutes and soon the pit bottom was full of men going out on strike.

The deputy manager ran down the gate to catch me up and plead once again to stop the walk out. But it was not in my gift to placate the manager – if union decisions, taken at national level, are ignored, there is no union.

After twenty-four hours the workforce returned to work all having lost one shift's pay. Not surprisingly, I was spot balled by management for the rag up and identified as a trouble-maker. Some NUM branch officials were also less than pleased by the hassle. Strikes caused them work. But at least I had stood my ground and the workforce responded by supporting the union position. What more can you ask?

The overtime ban had been the right tactic, a measured and effective response to closure threats, and it was putting pressure on the Coal Board without folks losing too much in the wage packet. But the NCB and government had other ideas and wanted to bring things to a head. They upped the stakes. Provocations from management were increasingly hard to ignore. Polmaise in Scotland came out on all-out strike. In South Yorkshire the matter was brought to a head at the Manvers complex.

Four pits were connected underground to the Manvers coal preparation and coking plant. Management, faced with the overtime ban, unilaterally introduced different shift and break (or snap) times to maximise production. It was a blatant attempt to reduce the effectiveness of the overtime ban, so the Manvers men walked out in late February 1984. Others at Wath Main were sent home without pay. A rolling strike with pickets pulled out all the pits in the complex and made preparations to take the strike to other pits.

For myself, I was in blissful ignorance of all this. Having planned a trip to the Lake District, I had no thoughts about pits or strikes that weekend. Walking the hills with snow drifts slowly thawing under stone walls allowed the mind to wander and finally relax. Scafell Pike in the distance, Skiddaw behind me – just take it all in. Strenuous exercise on the hills was therapy and cleared the head. An inner calm and satisfaction took over as I cast my gaze over crag and dale far into the distance back and forth. With a hint of spring in the air, why wouldn't this be the best place to be, away from the cares of work and trade union hassle?

Back home again on Sunday evening I quickly learned of the spreading dispute and that pickets had turned up on the pit lane. An emergency branch meeting was called. Things were moving fast but it was not clear if anyone was in control. I spoke in support of the rest of the South Yorkshire Panel pits. An older, quietly spoken collier formally put the motion to join the strike and was seconded by a fitter. The vote was carried overwhelmingly. Neither of these men has ever been allowed to forget that they started a strike that would last one year and one week.

By the end of that week the National Union made the area strikes official and called an all-out strike, citing the previous national ballot to try to stop a pit closure plan hatched by the NCB and government. Cortonwood colliery was the local pit under threat, but then so were many of the others. The 1984–1985 miners' strike had begun and no one knew what on earth they were getting into.

Coalfields are a mixture of urban and rural, and Nottinghamshire is more rural than most. Some of the pits were on the outskirts of the city of Nottingham, but the only other sizeable town is Mansfield. Many Nottinghamshire pits are surrounded by countryside with some main roads and also plenty of back roads. Sherwood Forest takes up a sizeable chunk of the coalfield area. It's not a long drive from South Yorkshire, but it can take time to get to grips with the local geography, especially in the middle of the night.

About half-a-dozen car loads of pickets from our pit travelled down in expectation of meeting the night shift going on, then hanging about until the day shift turned up at about four to five in the morning. A cold March wind blew through the car park of this Nottinghamshire pit, Bentinck. Pits look very similar throughout the UK and the blue and yellow paint job make it even harder to distinguish one from another. The winding gears are usually the best way to identify a colliery – they are all a bit different and some radically so.

Most of the car park was lit by sodium lighting but blue-white spotlights shone down around the pit itself. Visibility was not very good and figures occasionally moved in the shadows near the pit buildings. Many pit canteens and baths were built at the same time and the brick architecture was common across all coalfields.

A long picketing shift awaited us but it was early in the strike and our enthusiasm was not yet dented by boredom and a growing sense of futility. The police had yet to turn up in big numbers. In truth, that night the police had not turned up at all. Their intelligence systems were clearly not yet up and running. This was how it was supposed to be – miners asking other miners to respect picket lines and make the strike solid. Arguments were inevitable, but at least there could be a direct exchange of views.

"Come on lads, let's make the strike solid!"

"Come on, your pit will be the next to shut if we don't stick together!"

"Come on – at least stop and listen!"

"Please your soddin' selves then – see if I care," I muttered to myself. I shifted my cap from one side to the other, took it off and scratched my head

– there was to be a lot of scratching of heads to come.

Cars pulled into the car park and dark figures scurried towards the canteen trying their best to ignore the pickets. Small groups of more friendly Nottinghamshire miners chatted with the pickets. Others threw their sandwiches to the pickets and drove home. If nothing else it was a good excuse for them to get back for the last pint at the club. Not all arse-licking Tories as you might think. Not yet a waste of time.

It is hard to point to any one reason for the attitude of many Notts and many other Midlands miners. There was history of strike breaking and being 'gaffers' men'. A separate union led by the Nottinghamshire Miners' Association General Secretary, George Spencer, was formed during the 1926 strike, breaking away from the Miners Federation and fatally weakening the strike efforts in the rest of the UK. This separate organisation stood cap in hand before their perceived 'betters'. Even affiliation to the Labour Party was rejected. Spencer himself switching from the Labour Party to the Liberal party. The separated organisation sought to accommodate itself with the coal owners and government of the day. After further local strikes and disturbances at Harworth in North Nottinghamshire, eventually the breakaway union re-affiliated to the national Miners' Federation in 1937.

In 1979 the productivity scheme re-introduced incentives and therefore huge wage differentials into the industry. Generally speaking, Nottinghamshire pits were highly productive and the miners earned more than many other parts of the UK. Some miners in the Midlands thought they were safe and pit closures were not their problem. The socialist traditions of the labour movement did not mean much to them. Their forefathers in the 1920s and 30s appeared to have set the tone.

I always found it hard to understand why working people ever voted Tory. Whatever negative thoughts people may have about governments, it's hard to grasp why anyone from coalfield communities would think the Tories are ever going to look out for them. The fall of the so-called 'Red Wall' in 2019 demonstrates the often complex relationship between those that rule and those who are ruled. 'Get Brexit Done' certainly appealed to many traditional Labour voters.

After most of the oncoming shift had either gone in to work or gone home, a lone figure wandered out from the canteen. Silhouetted by light from the canteen his face then came into view. In a strong Nottinghamshire accent, he greeted a group of pickets and, being the only NUM Committee man picketing, I walked over to speak with the man. I did not know at the time but this bloke was called Neil Greatrex.

"Evening lads, I'm an NUM Branch Official here. How's it all going then? There's been no trouble and we would like to keep it like that." He smiled nervously and glanced around.

"Now … look …" (He spoke quietly now.) "If you just back off and give my lads a chance it should turn out fine. We've got a meeting and I'm sure we can sort something out. We know the government want to shut pits and we understand the problem. We are on your side and we are in the same union."

The man seemed reasonable and had a grasp of the issues so no one had any reason to doubt his sincerity. He retraced his steps to the canteen and the pickets stood around hopeful. Things might be looking up, I allowed myself to think. If it's like this all over Nottinghamshire, Thatcher could be in for a shock.

Time ticked by and the Notts official never came out of the meeting. It was difficult to see in the half-light, but most of the men were now going into the pit baths and then presumably on to work. Two Notts men came in our direction. One of these lads became a friend of mine and a solid comrade through the strike and in battles yet to come.

"Sorry about this," the Nottinghamshire striker said shuffling his feet a little unsure how the pickets might react.

"That two-faced bastard just sold you down the river. He was the only union official at the meeting and he argued against strike action, slagged you all off for intimidation of his members and slated the NUM leadership. He even moved a motion of no confidence in Scargill. Most of 'em have gone in to work – sorry."

"I bet he can't lay in bed straight," one picket spluttered. "Fancy ... he had the cheek to talk to us and then shaft us ..."

"Lower than shark shit," said another.

"I told you, I told you – " another said, "back stabbers ..."

"Didn't like the look of him from the off, why did we listen to his bollocks?"

That very same NUM Official, Neil Greatrex, helped form the new breakaway outfit, the Union of Democratic Mineworkers or UDM. Lauded by Thatcher and her right-wing Tory sycophants, they would actively work to break the strike and try to do a deal to save their own pits – the Spencer union re-born. There was no deal on offer as later closures were to show. Thatcher was pissing up their backs but they were too stupid and too grasping to realise it.

The same man was later elected to President of the UDM. The formation of this breakaway was driven often by personal greed by its leading officials. Shadowy figures, like David Hart, who had a close working relationship with Thatcher, provided covert support to the breakaway organisation.[41]

The federated structure of the NUM meant that most of the funds resided in the areas and Nottinghamshire was one of the bigger areas. The UDM President enjoyed the patronage of Tory ministers and had no real work to do because his so-called union had no role beyond collecting subscriptions. He could bank his large monthly salary from a diminishing membership as Nottinghamshire and other Midlands pits closed in the lead up to and after privatisation. They thought themselves 'big fish', but in very little ponds that were drying up fast.

Not content with this cushy job, much later in 2012, Greatrex found himself imprisoned having been found guilty of stealing funds supposed to go to the retired miners' home in Skegness. Grasping and small-minded, he demonstrated the selfishness and unworthiness of the UDM leadership. They had nothing to offer, sitting back whilst the industry was butchered. They looked after themselves and their cronies. Not surprisingly, their political

---

41 See Ramsay: *The British Gladio and the murder of Sergeant Speed* Lobster 2021 – Civil Contingencies Cadre.

patrons soon dropped them off their Christmas card list. No pride, no dignity and a lasting disgrace to the coal mining industry.

That first night in Nottinghamshire the pickets had some success, but it was difficult to assess just how many men had turned back and even harder to know what the real level of support was. Most of the pickets were holed up in their cars for a long cold night, but the enterprising younger lads went scavenging for wood and coal. The ubiquitous brazier was now burning and casting a flickering light across the car park providing warmth for cold hands.

Well before dawn a busload of police turned up and fanned out across the pit entrance. An inspector confronted the pickets across the road.

"Any attempt to stop men going on shift, speak to them or interfere in any way, will result in immediate arrest," he told those near enough to hear.

Emerging in dribs and drabs from the cars, the rest of the pickets joined their mates in front of the line of police. Not fancying the odds, they stood making a few gestures and half-heard appeals for support as the day shift went in to work. Some lads turned around and threw their snap to the Yorkshire pickets. A bit of breakfast at least, but not much else to be cheery about.

Turning to leave and disheartened by their night's experience, two men approached the pickets – Nottinghamshire strikers with news.

"A picket has been killed at Ollerton … Lots of your mates from other pits are trying to get there."

"I just don't believe this – what the fuck is happening?" I uttered quietly through gritted teeth. Any number of scenarios flashed across my tired mind. The pickets looked at each other and in one voice said:

"Where the fuck is Ollerton?"

It was light and clear when we arrived in Ollerton village. Where's the pit? Not difficult to spot after a short walk – it was surrounded by rank on rank of police. There were plenty of pickets too, but most were standing about looking lost. No one knew what was happening and no one knew what had happened. There was tension in the air and the least provocation could have started a riot, but following the death of a fellow miner, even the most lairy of pickets made some attempt to be calm and dignified.

Picket killed? How and by who? The questions repeated time after time in everyone's head. All kinds of rumours and inaccurate stories circulated through the gathering crowd, any basis in truth becoming less likely as time went on. The established account later became just as inconclusive. David Jones, was a young miner from South Kirkby, but worked at Acton Hall colliery near Featherstone. His family were part of the Welsh diaspora as was mine – his father, Mark, never losing his Welsh accent.

Not long after the mass of police had turned up on 15 March 1984, David was said to have received a blow on the chest. He died in hospital some hours later. Who or what was responsible for his death was never legally established. An open verdict stands to this day. The truth was conspicuous by its absence once again. Mistrust and suspicion filled in the gap left between truth and lies.

There was nothing more to do, the show of strength had been noted and an unofficial truce took over from all the frantic action. Shock and disbelief resulted in calm resignation and even the police knew when to keep a lid on it. The tired, and quietly alarmed pickets made their way back to their cars and drove north. Each one of them way out of their comfort zone, struggling to make sense of a very new and shocking experience. What was happening? What had we stumbled into and what was to become of us all, and the strike?

Another miner was killed a little later on in the strike. Joe Green was on the brink of retiring when the strike started. As he stood peacefully outside a power station gates, a forty-tonne truck cut the corner and ran its back wheels over him. Perhaps yet another 'Act of God.'

For many years there were annual demonstrations to mark these deaths. To this day the memories and lives of David Jones and Joe Green are celebrated at a gathering in the Miners Hall in Barnsley in early March.

The massive police invasion of the Nottinghamshire and other midlands coalfields was unprecedented. This wasn't in the Arthur Scargill book of strike action. As scary as it was in those first days and weeks, the police siege and occupation were to become a way of life for months. People can get used to most things, but being inured to aggression, violence and threats shouldn't excuse it. The level of violence increased in proportion to the level of police intervention.

This was a new type of strike – free collective bargaining by civil disobedience on the part of the miners and negotiation by truncheon on the part of the police. Rioting became a police pastime as officers from up and down the UK travelled far and wide, dished out state-sponsored good hidings and picked up wads of overtime pay.

For my crew it took a little while to sink in. Yet as the days and weeks passed, we adjusted to the new reality – roadblocks, mouthy coppers, conflict and threats. It dawned on us that there was a limit to what could be done in the circumstances and the hopes and ambition to win the strike quickly were soon lost in the tit-for-tat war with the police. It was easy to weary of this futile daily battle – the bigger the battle the more media coverage. Media coverage became an end in itself – stopping coal production was secondary. Anger and indignation kept me and my mates' engines running despite the head-banging, confusion and emotional torments.

Adrenaline, bowls of soup and cups of tea fuelled the body. The soul was fed by the people who stood by the miners against all the odds. The thousands of women involved in the villages and the Women Against Pit Closures movement stood shoulder to shoulder with us, convincing us in our darkest moments that it was all worth it and it was possible to win. Losing your own self-respect, being a strike breaker, was unthinkable.

Other strikers conceded after weeks of stalemate that they had better things to do and that usually meant looking after their families. Some local councils provided financial help via the social services for dependents but, with no wage coming in for men, things got very difficult.

Some lads made the effort to get out of bed and pick up their £1 picketing fee plus petrol money. But at the first road block they would turn around and go home. Those who had the opportunity took jobs on the side. Some became house-husbands allowing their wives to do a full-time job, perhaps for the first time. Everyone had some survival strategy to fall back on. There was no judgment made; stopping out on strike was all that was asked of them. Eventually the pressures led to doubt and desperation. Egged on by NCB propaganda, and in many cases personal approaches, individual miners cracked.

But this only began to happen in the autumn of the strike in Yorkshire, months after the enthusiasm and hope had faded as negotiations between the NCB and NUM leaders were scuppered by unseen hands time and time again. For the likes of me and the strike activists, the time arrived to up the ante and take the fight to the police occupation of the coalfields. Pressure was put on the NUM leadership to organise bigger pickets to raise the profile of the strike in the media and give Thatcher something to worry about. Larger numbers of pickets were concentrated at target pits.

Almost every day the television had scenes of mayhem up and down the Midlands coalfields. Massed police or not, this strike was going on and bugger the consequences. The weeks went by and the mileage built up quickly: Immingham Docks, Agecroft, Babbington, Parsonage, Cresswell, Mansfield, Rufford, Bilsthorpe, Blidworth, Calverton, Cadley Hill, Harworth, Cotgrave, Ratcliffe power station – the names and places became a blur.

The active pickets began to operate independently often beyond the official instructions. A day shift target of one pit might be stopped by police roadblocks so they went elsewhere if they found a way through. Miners from different panels and areas were in communication trying to out-fox the police who often seemed to know what was planned. It was likely information did leak from union officials in Barnsley or at some point in the command chain. Undercover operations did not emerge as a real story until decades later.

Despite the huge police presence, the numbers on strike stayed solid and coal production in the Midlands coalfields was well down. This was a high point of the strike in terms of numbers not going to work, but it could not be sustained without some hope of concluding the strike.

Many hard-core strikers, including myself, thought another ballot for strike action could have been won, thus taking away any excuses from the doubters. It seemed we would have nothing to lose and everything to win. Yet the fear was that a ballot would give the media the chance to influence the membership. Surely, some of us thought, the TUC and others would act if the NUM took the high ground? Many others, including Scargill, were not prepared to take the chance. There was no second ballot, so we just dug in and hoped.

Talks at national level were a roller coaster of high expectations followed by disappointment. It was unlikely there was any real intention by Thatcher and McGregor to do a deal with the NUM. Hopes were deliberately raised, it seemed, just to be crushed with a breakdown in talks the day after. This had the desired effect and the number of Midlands strikers fell as individuals, seeing no end to the dispute and mortgages to pay, threw in the towel.

Where the strike remained solid, the doubts and pressure to return to work were much less. Being on strike when most of your pit was working was the hardest position to be in.

The strike had a peculiar geography based in some part on history, but also on work 'culture'. Nottinghamshire, Leicestershire, South Derbyshire and Warwickshire were the weaker areas for the strike. South Wales was the strongest. Areas such as Lancashire, and Staffordshire had majority support but also a minority who defied the strike. Scotland was largely solid with the odd strike breaker. The North East was also solid with some strike breakers keeping pickets busy. Derbyshire was mixed, with the influence of the nearby Nottinghamshire strike breakers ever present.

Yorkshire was strongest at its core towns like Barnsley and Doncaster. The nearer you got to Nottinghamshire the more the cracks began to show in the autumn and winter. Thurcroft pit was only a few miles from the Nottinghamshire and Derbyshire borders. The new Selby coalfield also began to return in bigger numbers late on in the strike.

The body of men who were prepared to defy their own trade union became a breeding ground for anti-union discontent. The NCB and Government seized on this and began to build a 'fifth column' that would eventually split the union and hand the industry over to Tory policies.

7

"TAKE PRISONERS!" – THE BATTLES AT ORGREAVE

The news was that lorries were taking coke from the British Steel coking plant at Orgreave near Sheffield to supply the big steel works over in Scunthorpe. South Yorkshire was the main supplier of coking coal to the steel industry. Scunthorpe was Thurcroft colliery's main customer and Treeton colliery supplied the coke works at Orgreave.

A trainload of coal from Cortonwood – the pit that nominally started the national strike – had been allowed to go to Scunthorpe with the blessing of the mining and rail unions as a gesture of solidarity with the steel workers. A deal had been struck to allow enough coal and coke for Scunthorpe to keep its blast furnaces ticking over and prevent any long-term damage. This had been the deal in previous strikes.

I dropped in on a couple of pickets at Orgreave on my way home from Nottinghamshire one lunchtime. Sure enough, a convoy of full trucks had left earlier that day.

"Bleedin' marvellous – we are dragging our arses around every coalfield in the country and they are moving coke right under our noses in South Yorkshire," I growled to myself spitting out every word.

It didn't take long for the situation at Orgreave to be on every picket's lips – a kick in the teeth from the leaders of the steel unions; a provocation; a government set-up that could not go unchallenged. NUM Branch officials at our pit were asked to report back to Barnsley HQ that the concession of coal and coke for Scunthorpe was at an end and every effort should be made to halt the convoys. Unless something was done about Orgreave, the pickets would desert and the strike would implode. The common belief, or gripe, was that following orders from Barnsley had got them nowhere – why bother picketing in Nottinghamshire if the strike was being defeated in South Yorkshire?

Each day after a shift picketing in Nottinghamshire and elsewhere, Yorkshire pickets drove back to South Yorkshire. On more than one occasion they had a bit of a laugh on the motorway. With three picketing cars abreast, it was possible to cause huge traffic jams by all slowing to fifteen miles an hour. Pickets had done this on the Humber Bridge to great effect and the tactic caught on. The objective was simply to disrupt where they could and cause the police a headache.

It wasn't without its dangers. Travelling north one day on the M1 a scab coal wagon decided to break the slow time blockade. He drove like a madman up the hard shoulder with a forty-tonne truck. He got away with it and it demonstrated to the pickets that some drivers weren't just doing it for money, they seemed to have had a personal hatred of the striking miners.

At the Orgreave coking plant it was possible early on to stand next to the gates and push the police when the convoy arrived. But it did not take long before the police took out their truncheons. I was a couple of rows back when the front of the 'scrum' collapsed. Nearly taken down, I held on to a lad in front of me holding him up as best I could under both arms. Whack! A black-gloved fist bounced off my nose. I could not defend myself with both arms holding the fallen picket.

The confrontation broke up and I staggered back, blood streaming down my face. My mates took a look and asked for medical assistance. The First Aid Station at the coking plant was next to the entrance gates and with one mate

I was allowed in for attention. A first aid man in a white coat looked gruffly at my blood splattered face. He cleaned me up with some sterile wipes and gave me a handful of lint and cotton wool.

"I don't think it's broke … you should be OK," the medic offered as reassurance.

"Broke? Jesus … I don't want to end up looking like some washed up boxer! Let's have a look … "

I found a mirror and stared at the offending nose.

My mate burst out laughing.

"You're in a battle with the fucking police and all you are worried about is your pretty face … yer knob head!" he blurted out, barely able to stop a snigger. Back on the picket line other mates chipped in with yet more piss taking.

The police officer who thumped me turned up as an arresting officer at a Magistrates' Court hearing for another picketing incident some weeks later. We were there supporting other strikers on charges. The cocky young officer spotted me at the same time as I clocked him. He had a laugh with his mates in blue.

"I'll see you around again no doubt, pal," said the copper.

"I bet you will," I replied, itching to give him a mouthful but thinking better of it. The full name, number and police station of that copper, read out in court, are etched in my brain to this day.

Many people may find it hard to believe just how unpleasant some of these police were. In contrast, a young police officer deployed in the strike and at Orgreave was to train as a teacher. He found himself many years later teaching my youngest daughter. The class touched on the miners' strike as any history class would do once it was far enough back in time. She told the class her dad had been a miner on strike. After the class the teacher, and former police officer, approached her and apologised – no doubt he was young and a bit green. Others played their part with much more relish.

For a few weeks the pickets made their way each day to Orgreave to confront the truck convoys. It wasn't 'official' action but the numbers demonstrated to the NUM hierarchy that these daily battles could not be ignored. And they were battles. The level of aggravation escalated to the highest in the strike so far. Riot police and mounted police charges became the norm.

Any chatty local bobby was replaced by a colleague trained in riot tactics. This was their chance to behave like state-sponsored football hooligans – no holds barred.

The NUM National President, Arthur Scargill, turned up without invitation from Barnsley Area NUM HQ. Say what you like about Arthur, but he liked picketing and was hooked on the notion that the victory at Saltley Gates in the 1972 strike could be repeated at Orgreave. He was in the thick of it in a US miners' baseball cap urging the lads to try and stop the convoys. He got arrested and the national news was full of it. If nobody had heard of Orgreave before – they had now.

Arthur had also been arrested on a demonstration in support of the Grunwick strikers in 1976. His trips to the Magistrates' and law courts built his reputation. Arthur was the target of the right-wing press for decades and he was quick to use the law whenever he could to defend himself. From my point of view there was not always much merit in this course of action as the focus was inevitably on Scargill himself rather than the issues.

The Yorkshire Area NUM leadership wanted to take the steam out of the clashes at Orgreave and for a while everything went quiet. Routine picketing elsewhere continued but at the Yorkshire Miners' Gala in Wakefield on Saturday 16 June 1984 the rumour went around that there would be a national picket at Orgreave on Monday 18 June. It would be the first, and last, nationally organised picket of the strike.

The day broke warm and sunny. At the height of summer, the sun was up very early and so were the birds. At any other time, most people would consider themselves blessed to be walking the streets, lanes and countryside on such a fine day.

For my part, this was an almighty cock-up. My aging Fiat Mirafiori had given up the ghost. My old Italian associates at Fiat car plants did not make cars to last. I was in the process of replacing the back axle – a big job for someone with no car mechanical training – but I had no wages. I knew the orders for the day through contacts in the NUM National Office, but with no car, I couldn't get to my own pit to be deployed and join my mates. I got the push bike out and gave it the once over then set off for Orgreave, which was only a couple of miles over the hills of east Sheffield.

At the bottom of the hill coming down from Handsworth I decided to ditch the bike and casually launched it over a hedge – no one would see it there I concluded. I made my way to the top end of the lane that runs down to the coke works entrance over a railway bridge. Wide open fields on one side, a wall and scruffy workshops on the other and a rail line beyond. Railways also to my back and along one side, but not the main line.

It was later than I wanted to be but, despite the gathering crowds of pickets and massed police ranks down at the entrance, the air was full of light-hearted chat and songbirds competing together in the morning air. For the first time in the strike the Yorkshire lads were joined by Scottish, Welsh, Durham and Northumberland miners, few of whom had the slightest idea what they had let themselves in for. This, in some of their minds was just a demonstration, a parade of support for the strike.

Unable to join my mates over the pit tip at the back of the coke works, I found some Barnsley Panel lads and my brother. Chatting and joking, it was like a day out in the sun.

Mass picketing was often a ritualistic affair – ranks of miners pushing lines of police. Not much different to a very big rugby scrum. The trouble is the police did not want to play; they were taking it much more seriously.

A few shoves from the pickets and the coppers began to buckle. They got the wind up and out came the truncheons, lashing out at arms and legs and occasionally heads. My brother caught a blow from a truncheon that split his forehead and he was dragged out of the melee by fellow pickets. As with all head wounds, there was plenty of blood and, after some unprofessional wiping with a hanky, a gash was found. It might need stitches so my brother took off up the field and eventually made his way to A&E in Sheffield in his car. He would return later with an impressive head bandage.

The main mass of pickets pulled back from the police and the scene returned once more to banter and the odd insult. The day was now heating up as the morning progressed and many pickets began to just sit about and take in the sun.

Without any warning, the police ranks opened and mounted police came charging at us up the hill. Behind the horses were the short-shield snatch squads wielding truncheons.

"Take prisoners Mr Simpson!" bellowed the police commander, dressed like Darth Vader.

Many of the miners from other areas stood and stared. Yorkshire lads ran up the hill towards the railway cutting. Scuffles and arrests occurred where miners had not taken evasive action. After about fifteen minutes the police fell back behind their long shield lines and the dispersed pickets tried to get re-orientated. The police now sent out their message rhythmically banging their shields and the low rumble carried across the fields. I don't suppose that was in the training manual.

The South Yorkshire and Doncaster Panel pickets had been deployed to the back of the coking plant and came over the old pit tip. Unseen by the rest of the pickets up the hill, a huge battle took place on the plant itself. Squinting in the sun, it was possible to see pickets and police tumbling over walls and spilling into the road below the plant entrance.

Police dogs had been deployed indiscriminately and the unprepared police reacted with more violence than usual – it was a free-for-all. I had not fully appreciated it at the time, but many of the arrests that were made during these confrontations on the plant were the ones that were to receive riot and affray charges later on.

Another cavalry charge followed by short-shield snatch squads had most pickets running back up the hill again, down into the railway cutting and up the other side. We all milled around garages, workshops and the ASDA supermarket next to houses. Tripping into front gardens and down any nook and cranny available, the pickets were pursued now by the police on horseback and those in full riot gear. An ice cream van – *Rock on Tommy* – featured in many photographs of the scene.

The police retreated and took up an impregnable position on the narrow road bridge over the railway line. Long shields at the front, backed up by armoured Range Rovers, the police had cleared all the pickets from near the coking plant and the convoys of trucks had a free hand to come and go.

Small groups of pickets began to erect their own defences. The key thing was to stop the horses. They had done this some weeks earlier with a burning Portacabin, now they resorted to tearing down an old stone wall along the side of the road. They built piles of stones and placed fencing poles in the centre angled at any advancing horses. Not much of a deterrent, but enough to stop an all-out charge. A feeble but smoky burning barricade was hastily built. Debris in the road and smoke gently rising in the heat of the day.

The pickets had run out of ideas and energy. All the police needed to do was hang around behind their shields. Eventually the pickets dispersed in small groups, some hanging back to hurl insults, but it was only gestures at this late stage. After all, they had not stopped the convoys.

For those arrested the shit was only just beginning. Miles away in police cells miners who had been arrested that day were being fitted up with riot and affray charges and potentially facing life in prison.

I found my bandaged brother and then the pushbike. I took the front wheel off, put it in my brother's Ford Escort and we drove back to Sheffield. There was still plenty of the day left and we called in at a town centre pub for a pint. The sight of a bloke with a head bandage walking up to the bar resulted in a few raised eyebrows and stares, but no one commented. Apart from those directly involved and a few ASDA shoppers, no one as yet knew what had happened just a few miles away that nice summer day.

The evening television news was full of images of violent clashes and the government and police were well positioned to transmit their version of this episode into the public consciousness.

The 'Battle of Orgreave' was to go down in folklore. Films and re-enactments were made and younger people asked ex-miners, 'Were you at Orgreave?' I suspect the answer was yes even if they had never been near the place. Funny thing, years after the NUM's power was broken, lots of people seemed to finally see the injustice of it all. Perhaps they found out they had a second cousin or an uncle who once worked down a pit. A misty-eyed nostalgia took over and miners were once again the 'salt of the earth' rather than 'the enemy within' as Thatcher had claimed. No point in knocking this nostalgia, but we really needed other trade unions to join in with sympathetic strikes or any form of industrial action at the time. That's when it would have really mattered and possibly led to a very different outcome in history.

Many of the arrested miners were charged with riot, unlawful assembly and affray. This was the way of the British law system. If the law was still on the statute book from the Tolpuddle Martyrs back to the English Civil War and well before, you could charge some poor unsuspecting bugger with it and lock them up for thirty years.

The later trial of those arrested on 18 June at Orgreave could have been a farce on the West End stage, but the possible consequences were not funny. The justification of the leading prosecuting QC for the repeated charges by riot and mounted police was 'the indiscriminate *shelling*' of police lines. In my head I was on the Somme but in truth Orgreave was more like Agincourt or Rourke's Drift. Indiscriminate shelling? You couldn't help but laugh – what was this highly paid legal gobshite talking about? Everybody, not just me, seemed to be back on the Western Front.

If support was lacking from some trade union leaders and the Labour leadership during and after the strike, it was not the case from some progressives in the legal profession. Solicitors and barristers for the defendant miners rallied around. They soon spotted who was doing the conspiring. The fabrications were routine and blindingly obvious. They wiped the floor with the concocted stories from the police. Statements had been dictated to arresting officers by CID colleagues, who had been sitting in an office nowhere near Orgreave. A host of other illegal activities were also exposed and the state was forced to drop the serious charges.

The same South Yorkshire police tried a re-run of this fanciful storytelling after the Hillsborough football ground disaster in 1989. The outcome decades later demonstrates just how the powers-that-be close ranks and cover up. South Yorkshire police came under further scrutiny many years after because of their failure to act to protect girls from sexual exploitation in the Rotherham area.

Much later, some financial compensation was awarded for the arrested victims of Orgreave, but the truth never saw the light of day and justice is yet to be served. The big unanswered question was just how much the state – the police and government in the main – had been the ones doing the conspiring. Conspiracy and cock-up theories are almost interchangeable, but the outcome was much the same for Orgreave. You could not help thinking we had walked into a trap set deliberately to intimidate anyone prepared to question Tory rule.

This legal setback was a fair price to pay for the police and the Government.

They had done what they set out to do: intimidate the NUM, the striking miners and anyone who might support them. Going on strike and challenging the state was, in effect, illegal. You now faced not only physical assaults, fines and the sack, but you could go to jail for thirty years. We got the message.

Perhaps just as important, from the government's point of view, the NUM and its officials had to step back and take stock – what had they got their members in to? They had not signed up for this – it was beyond their experience.

After months of picketing, the burden on the NUM, in terms of dealing with arrested, jailed and later sacked members, grew and grew. It had a direct impact on the lads involved of course, but also on the organisation of the strike. Once arrested and charged, miners were subject to court rulings that stopped them picketing. All the police had to do was arrest as many miners as possible to whittle down the numbers picketing. Then there was all the hassle and headache of court proceedings, which bogged down the union in a swamp of administration.

The day was often picketing early morning – hassle, abuse, disappointment – then Magistrates' court to support a few mates facing charges. The strike was sucked into activities related to the police and legal system and rarely the business of getting the message across to other trade unions and building support throughout the country. We were on strike, yes, and battling everything thrown at us, but failed to stop coal production in the Midlands or coal distribution to the power and steel industries

If Orgreave was a test of resolve or nerve, the NUM were the first to blink. The NUM Yorkshire Area leadership were intimidated by potential consequences for the union and for the members. The only responsible way forward for them was to calm things down. Orgreave never saw further mass picketing again and the battles of the strike, of which there were many, were fought elsewhere.

I sometimes thought I was in a minority of one, but my view about Orgreave was that the main mistake was not going back on June 19, 20, 21 – as long it took to either stop the trucks or bring so much pressure on the government they had to back off. You just keep coming back. You don't need to be violent, just relentless.

We had plenty of ideas about how to stop a convoy of trucks, some of them downright dodgy. Yet we stuck to the mass picket tactic and played into the hands of a very organised police force. It seemed obvious that new tactics were needed to break the stalemate but there was no official avenue in the union to convey this message to the leadership. The problem was simple enough: when hundreds of miners together are confronted by riot police there is only one possible outcome – a riot. Time and time again a peaceful picket would turn nasty just because the riot police turned up.

I can recall a warm day in August 1984 in the open fields surrounding one of the Selby pits. It was a two Panel picket so there were maybe a couple of hundred pickets and maybe twenty police in normal uniforms. An inspector approached the lads and we chatted for short while.

"Nothing much happening," we said to him.

"We will be gone in an hour." I reassured the officer.

In the distance a column of police riot vans came down the long lane from the main road. The police intelligence had been slow on the uptake that morning and presumably this mass picket had not been expected.

That's blown it, I thought as the police piled out and advanced like Roman legions towards us. The pickets were going to be corralled in so they scarpered across the fields turning as one after fifty metres or so to launch clods of earth at the new arrivals. The air was thick with lumps of ploughed earth clattering down on the police lines like a flock of starlings. It was time to get out and the pickets took various routes across the open ground to get to their cars.

Two police Transit vans were parked half way down the lane. With twenty blokes on each van, the pickets flipped them over on their roofs, leaving them wheels up and stranded in the fields like up-turned beetles.

If you wanted a riot, the quickest way to start one was to send in the riot police. It was a pattern it was difficult to get out of. Other tactics, at least from the pickets' point of view, never got a look in.

The widespread use of riot police and the consequent escalation of violence and public disorder came as shock during the miners' strike. It should not have done. The police were gearing up for this type of confrontation for some years.

It wasn't that the police were ever particularly friendly; I was familiar with good hidings from the police some fourteen years before the 84 miners' strike. An anti-Vietnam War protest in Barnsley ended up with me being bounced off the four walls of a police cell. The policeman was a veteran of the Korean War and did not like communists. I was charged with being 'Drunk and Disorderly' and fined £4 in a magistrates' court. A political prisoner of sorts I suppose, but hardly the stuff of legends.

The militarisation of the police could be tracked back to the sixties and seventies, when the experience of the police in Northern Ireland began to influence the use of modern hardware and training.

The Special Patrol Group (SPG) built a reputation in London attacking demonstrations. A young New Zealander and teacher, Blair Peach, was killed by a crushing blow to the head. The finger pointed to the SPG but they escaped any blame. The verdict was 'Death by misadventure.' Yet one more 'Act of God' perhaps.

Thirty-one years later a report from a Met Commander appeared at last in the public domain stating very clearly: an officer, or officers, in the SPG were to blame. The Metropolitan Police issued an apology but no one was ever charged.

In industrial disputes, the use of riot police first made its mark in the Stockport Messenger dispute. Riot police were used to break up protests led by the print unions resisting job losses in 1983. The dispute was still going when the miners' strike started.

A leaflet of the National Graphical Association (NGA) from the time read: 'Solidarity not sympathy is what we need.' A prequel perhaps to what the miners also needed and did not get enough of.

In the aftermath of the New Cross fire in South London, black communities had had enough. The 1981 riots in Brixton, Liverpool and elsewhere saw the police fully take on their paramilitary role. This was a big change in policing. They were prepared and up for it. Indeed, the police appeared to revel in this new paramilitary role.

The 'accidental deaths' of dozens of black people, mainly young men, go on to this day. The institutional racism of the police appears to know no shame. Misogyny and racism can be found in most sections of society, but its apparently high incidence rate amongst the very people we wish to trust to protect people, and society, is deeply disturbing.

Just after the miners' strike, a convoy of new age travellers tried to get to Stonehenge for the Solstice in June 1985. They were stopped and brutally dealt with by truncheon-wielding coppers in the 'Battle of the Beanfield'. The scenes of young people, sometimes with little kids, being knocked to the ground in a field of green beans even shocked the Home County Tories.

In October of the same year, Broadwater Farm erupted in Tottenham. Violence reached new heights with the death of a police officer.

Back in the industrial arena the Wapping dispute of 1986, once again with the print unions resisting job losses, saw more riot police in action.

There are many more examples of government-backed police thuggery and even more examples of individual policemen who abused their power for their own personal gratification. If anything, by the 2020s, it got worse not better, despite the promises of reform. The *Dixon of Dock Green* image of the police lay in tatters. The Thatcher government can take much of the responsibility for the erosion of public consent. There is, we were told, 'No such thing as society'. Inequality and injustice were increasingly state sponsored.[42]

The downstream consequences of Orgreave and the dozens of other confrontations was the building of long-term campaigns to defend the striking miners, their families and seek some justice. A South Yorkshire Defence Campaign – Jobs not Jail – was started by striking miners and Women Against Pit Closures with help from people in the legal profession in the last few months of the strike. The government, through the police and courts, had used every possible law from Breach of the Peace to Conspiracy to Riot with one aim in mind – to intimidate striking miners and their supporters. It was huge task just keeping up with the court appearances in South Yorkshire never mind across the UK.

---

42 The process of 'militarisation' of the police is meticulously and very well documented in the book by Foot M. & Livingstone M. Charged – *How the Police Try to Suppress Protest*. 2022.

The South Yorkshire Defence Campaign continued for some years after the return to work, dealing with victimised miners. The Jobs Not Jail banner still appears from time to time at the annual Orgreave rally and Durham Miners' Gala.

Justice for Mineworkers was set up to support nearly a thousand miners sacked as a result of strike activity. The organisation continues to this day raising money. It is not part of popular consciousness, but over three hundred miners remained sacked. The Labour Government in 2001 conceded an enhanced pension entitlement for some of these. But this hardly compensated for a life sentence for standing up to Thatcher.

Decades later, spurred on by the campaign to uncover the truth about the Hillsborough football disaster, the Orgreave Truth and Justice Campaign continued the work to reveal the truth about Orgreave and expose the illegal and mendacious actions of the then Tory government. The Westminster Government has refused to carry out an Inquiry. However, in 2020 the Scottish Government pardoned Scottish miners convicted in the 84–85 strike. The Westminster Government however, dug its heels in and refused to take a further look at the strike, and in particular Orgreave. A debate in Parliament in June 2022 raised many familiar questions but the Minister stonewalled yet again.[43]

A much broader inquiry into Undercover Policing was started in 2015. Its stated purpose was 'to get to the truth about undercover policing across England and Wales since 1968 and provide recommendations.' The NUM took the opportunity to make its case with regard to policing of the miners' strike.[44] That inquiry rumbles on. With over fifty years of policing to cover, at the time of writing, it is unlikely to report any time soon. Inevitably there may be much more we have yet to find out about the dirty tricks deployed by the state in the affairs of trade unions and any other group or individuals defending their rights.

Maybe that inquiry will also cover the 'secret state conspiracy' to arrest,

---

43 *Miners' Strike 1984–85: UK-wide Inquiry*. Hansard, Volume 717, 29 June 2022.
44 Opening Statement on behalf of the National Union of Mineworkers to the Undercover Policing Inquiry. 26 October, 2020.

convict and blacklist building workers during and after their national strike back in 1972. The government, media and shadowy 'anti-communist' organisations are once again in the spotlight.⁴⁵

After the spectacular pitched battle at Orgreave, the strike settled into a steady slog – attrition, or the strike equivalent of trench warfare. The odd sortie, the occasional flare-up of hostilities with much the same result, except weeks had turned into months and some miners in the Yorkshire coalfield were feeling the strain.

The NCB, under orders from Downing Street, having nurtured an anti-NUM block in the Midlands coalfields, turned to Yorkshire. Systematically, individuals were identified that might break the strike. At first carefully orchestrated, scabs went back in vehicles covered in steel mesh under heavy police escort; first at one pit and then another. The process started on the Nottinghamshire and Derbyshire border and crept north.

The result of this organised strike-breaking was mayhem. At each pit, where it became known a scab was going in, confrontations occurred in the pitch black before dawn. The scenes were chaotic and picketing was random and guerrilla – it was often difficult to work out what was going on down dark lanes with the occasional burning barricade. This occupation of pit villages by the police widened the conflict. It was no longer an industrial dispute; it was a confrontation out of anyone's control, including the NUM Area Officials. Pickets were still deployed, but many miners in pit villages took matters into their own hands.

There were dozens of smaller-scale 'Battles of Orgreave' and what they lacked in scale they made up for in viciousness. The general public had no idea of the level of warfare going on in the coalfields because it mostly happened in the dark away from media attention. This was the new normal: the daily outbreak of hostilities and tension that went on for weeks on end and few people outside the coalfields paid much attention. You might get

---

45 Tom Coburg: *The Canary*. 7 February 2021.

used to it, but where would it all end?

Back in the house and a chance to try and turn off. You assume you are safe. A knock at the door and I am briefly startled – "Don't answer it, play daft!" I tell myself.

Belfast or Barnsley? Derry or Doncaster? You weren't sure anymore as the dawn broke to find the streets littered with rubble and smoke clearing from a burnt-out car.

Dawn Breaking – September 1984. Acrylic on canvas.

© David J Parry.

8

FIGHTING LIKE GIRLS

A letter arrives on the door mat:

Tupperware Party, Bilsthorpe, all invited.

Nottinghamshire in cold half-light. Engines ticking over in a line of vehicles and the odd raised voice.

Two bored police men chat. Their breaths mingling in the chilly air:

"This strike is proving a Godsend," confessed Pete, hometown Basildon.

"How's that?" inquired Gary, home town Chelmsford, though he wasn't really interested in an answer from his police colleague.

"Cash, my friend. Lolly, spondulicks – overtime pay, yer dickhead," he informed his fellow constable.

"I've been promising 'her indoors' a holiday in Spain and now she can have two if she wants!"

"Oh I see … " Gary murmured (as if he gave a fuck).

A mist was swirling into a hollow to the left of the roadblock and the lights of the vehicles bounced back off it. Exhaust fumes added further to the morning mist.

"Gary, check the blue minibus three cars back!" This police officer was playing his part as best he could, unlike some of his mates who were still half asleep.

Blue Ford Transit, ten women – 'Sheffield Women's Technology Workshop' on the van side.

He wanders up as casual as he can manage.

"What are you ladies doing this time of the day? A bit early for bingo."

It's a well-known fact, all women up north play bingo.

He might as well have said "'Ello, 'ello, 'ello, what's going on here then?" But then he wasn't old enough to know the patter of the old-time coppers when you can't find your way home.

"Plods: don't you just love 'em?" whispers Janet, sitting in the second row of the mini-bus. She smiles and looks out of the window in the other direction. Conversation amongst the women fades to silence.

"Sheffield, that's in South Yorkshire innit?"

This bloke ought to be on *University Challenge* says Janet to herself, digging her nails into the seat.

The driver, Caroline, speaks her lines clearly and with no repetition, hesitation or deviation:

"Single parents' conference in Norwich. It's a long way so we needed an early start. We came down this road because there is a big queue back at the roundabout onto the A60."

Don't blather on, she says to herself. She doesn't.

The other officer's attention is taken by a car behind. Four blokes dressed up like extras in a Ken Loach film.

"Would you look at these charmers … Pete, let the minibus go – this is what we're after."

Pete waves the minibus on and joins his colleague in blue.

"Come on you tossers, get out and put yer hands on the car roof!" Gary is in his element playing Starsky and Hutch.

Fifty yards down the road the minibus is away and the ten women burst out laughing and some into song.

"Shove that where the sun don't shine" Janet says through gritted teeth. They all agree.

Onwards – Bilsthorpe Tupperware Party here we come!
"Here we go, here we go, here we go!"

Feminism was a familiar concept to men on the left. I had been active in left politics for many years and considered myself to be at least 'house trained' when it came to gender politics. For me, that often meant keeping my mouth shut and trying not to pontificate on the finer points of sexism and women's oppression. I was a bloke after all and the oppressor has no business directing the operations of the oppressed. Condescension comes easy to many men, especially on the left, with a head full of ideological and theoretical baggage. I always felt uneasy that this view was perhaps a cop-out but I think it stacks up.

The Women Against Pit Closures movement opened a new front in the strike and brought a whole new dimension to industrial action, protest, self-help and of course generally giving the NCB, police and government a hard time. The Government and NCB never quite got it – miners' wives and women supporters were the last thing on their mind when they provoked the strike in the first place.

Groups of women got themselves organised early on in the strike, in part as a reaction to the usual media coverage of strikers' wives. The *Daily Mail* version of a striker's wife was one that dragged her dozy husband back to work and taught him the good sense of earning money and ignoring his trade union. The priority for this type of women's movement was the mortgage payments and holidays in Marbella.

An oral history of transcribed tape recordings put together just after the strike conveys some of the feelings:

It was the first demonstration I'd been on. It wasn't what I expected at all. It was all women together. Everybody was applauding us. It was really uplifting … It was nice to belong to something and know that we all had something in common.

When we marched round Barnsley singing and shouting we enjoyed letting everyone know our feelings…..We couldn't get inside the theatre so sat on the grass and listened. The speeches were really moving. What stuck in my mind was one woman saying 'We are all in this together. We stand with our men, not just behind them, but with them on the front line.'[46]

Supported by women's groups from most cities and many towns, Labour Party constituencies and trade union branches from across the UK, the strikers' wives and families created a huge network outside any official structure. Its organising ability confounded the sceptics and its power had the potential to challenge the traditional labour movement hierarchy. Its main aim was to articulate the demands of the strike but it also built an ad-hoc, unofficial structure that could not be bought off and held the strike together when the going got really tough. Strikes historically had mainly been about terms and conditions for a particular group of workers. This strike was about the survival of communities and many women – wives, mothers, sisters or entirely unrelated – just got stuck in.

Food parcels and soup kitchens are often seen as the only type of activity the women's groups got involved in. After all, it was a traditional role that was based in the mining community history of strikes and hardships from 1926 and before. But the support and range of activities was much more. Speaking at meeting after meeting up and down the country – and internationally – the women raised awareness, support and hard cash. They stood up in mosques, Hindu and Sikh temples, chapels, synagogues and churches and explained the issues. They toured the country speaking to anyone prepared to listen. Women from our pit addressed meetings of hundreds of people.

Picket deployment for the striking miners came from orders originating in Barnsley. This passed down the Panels[47] and then to individual branches. I was deployed in the South Yorkshire Panel, and my brother in the Barnsley Panel. We both had a couple of sheets of paper with hand-written codes for each pit to exchange information on the phone. That way we would have

---

46 *Thurcroft. A Village and the Miners' Strike*. Gibbon & Steyne. 1986.
47 A sub-group of the NUM matching NCB areas in Yorkshire – there were four Panels at the time.

some notion about what was happening on any given morning. If both Panels were sent to the same target, then it could be classed as a 'mass' picket. We were no longer interested in small groups standing about being ignored.

There often seemed to be little rhyme or reason to the orders, but orders were orders. The women at least could be flexible and adapt their actions to what was actually happening on any particular day. The male pickets and the women pickets kept the police on the hop as much as possible, even if they did little to stop strike breakers.

The women were particularly adept at getting through roadblocks but the blokes were a sitting target. I tried to keep my partner, Caroline and her friends up-to-date with the road-block situation as best I could. But mobile phones were still science fiction in 1984.

There were some sneaky ways into Nottinghamshire but the police eventually got wise to most back routes. The Glapwell Gap from Derbyshire into Nottinghamshire via the Hardwick Hall country estate served pickets well, but it was not always reliable. Forest tracks were sometimes possible, but care had to be taken in the dark because of tree stumps.

One day, spotting a couple of plods on a single-track lane, we were forced to pull up. The police officer leaned into the car and spotted an OS Map on my mate's lap.

"Sergeant … sergeant … they've got maps!" gasped the officer.

Now, who would have thought that thick miners could read maps? As far as the sergeant knew there was no law against possessing maps – not yet. There were no laws stopping people driving into Nottinghamshire either but the police were happy to bend a few to suit their own ends.

If picketing miners or the women were not very successful at closing down the Midlands coalfields, the women were certainly an irritant to the bewildered police as they turned up to picket just as the weary police were hoping to be stood down and get a bit of breakfast.

Caroline was tirelessly active in the strike with Sheffield Women Against Pit closures. Two of my kids were around during the strike and featured from time to time. My eldest daughter Kate was six so will have her own memories. Her mother, Seni, was a former partner I had met at university. My little lad Tom, was a toddler in the strike, but my second daughter, Annie, was born later.

Tom was carried on shoulders to picket lines and demonstrations. He was perhaps too young to grasp what was going on at the time, but he had some part in history to recall to his own kids in turn. All three kids were familiar with the Branch banner on wheels that was pushed along at the Miners' Gala and other demonstrations. With a gang of other kids, they clung to the frame as the banner moved through the streets of pit towns.

Yet much of what my partner Caroline and I did in the strike was not done together. She spent a lot of time supporting the women in the pit village, going to meetings, demonstrations, picketing. But it was not my pit village, nor was it hers. We lived in the city some miles away and were not subjected to the daily aggravation of the besieged villages or the hardship and degraded local economy.

Caroline's activities with Women Against Pit Closures continued for many years and their activities took centre stage in 1992-93 when pit closures reached a climax.

She helped me try and piece it all together with some important history:

Barnsley Women Against Pit Closures was set up soon after the announcement of the strike, followed shortly afterwards by Sheffield Women Against Pit Closures. Flis and I initially joined Barnsley WAPC, then Sheffield where we lived. Sheffield was set up to support the women's groups in the seventeen local pits and two workshops in South Yorkshire.

The initial priority was to provide funds and food parcels to support families of striking miners. This was crucially important given the vindictive non-payment of benefits to single miners and the vicious cut of £15 in a family's social security benefit. We aimed to ensure no mining family would be starved back to work. But it wasn't long before the activities of Sheffield WAPC were as varied as its membership.

The first WAPC demonstration in South Yorkshire, in Barnsley on 12 May 1984, was impressive, and was testament to the importance women were to play in maintaining the strike over the following year. Our national WAPC demonstration in August of that year (11 August 1984) is something I will always be proud to have been a part of – it was led by women from the coalfields with determination and pride – as it was seven years later (February 1993).

Fundraising took on all forms. I remember, our son, Tom (then only 18 months old) bursting into tears as he saw me dressed up as a clown high up on stilts raising funds walking down Fargate. This was not the mum he knew! Over the year, women took on many roles – we went to Orgreave, and from then onwards took part in picketing – the women from the villages across South Yorkshire were keen to be involved, and so was I. I borrowed my work place's minibus, and collected any women wanting to come from Dave's pit and other pit villages close by. We were sent invitations to local 'Tupperware parties' in Nottinghamshire, and went off to support our sister WAPC groups there, aiming to get to the location of the 'party'.

I'd get a bit of advice on the best route from Dave as he returned home from early morning picketing. We had a laugh – important when so much made you want to weep or scream. We concocted all sorts of stories as we hit the police lines – we were off to a single parent conference, potato picking or whatever one of the women in the back of the minibus decided was the favourite of that particular trip. Supporting the women from Notts was very important, given the isolation of striking families there, and the efforts the government made to encourage the so-called Union of Democratic Mineworkers.

Whilst we were as serious as you can be – it was the survival of whole communities we were fighting for – we had justice on our side and would not give up. But we had a laugh as well – and made unexpected and wonderful friendships.

I had seen first-hand the racism of the Met Police whilst living in Brixton in the 1970s, but for many women the behaviour of the police was a shock. And it certainly put in perspective the many stories told by women and men coming to South Yorkshire from areas across the country offering support. Injustices were suffered by so many from marginalised communities – black and ethnic minority communities, gay communities and others who had for years been victimised by the police.

We all learnt a lot during that year, and whilst we lost the struggle, our history and the experience of so many women across all the coalfields will never be stamped out and will continue to inspire women everywhere. I am proud to have been a small part of it.

She was in good company. Woman Against Pit Closures, in all the various groups across the coalfields, stand out as a beacon of how it is possible to come together and challenge the powers that be. The groups emerged with no formal structures and organised everything from scratch. They were not hide-bound by suffocating procedures. Digging deep into real 'human resources' they were not hampered by hierarchies nor set in their ways.

During the strike, the women, not surprisingly, 'fought like girls,'[48] – fighting like men was getting NUM pickets nowhere.

---

48 *Fight Like a Girl*, Kalie Shorr, 2016.

Thurcroft picket – Women Against Pit Closures.

9

AGAINST ALL THE ODDS – HANGING ON

Although picketing hogged the headlines as Orgreave came and went, the self-help activities of striking communities took on a bigger, and in many ways, more important role. Survival strategies often come as second nature to most working-class families, but now it was whole communities that were moved to act.

Once more my relationship with pit villages was tested and found wanting. I went the thirteen miles there to work, to union meetings and occasionally to socialise, but that was about it. I was well known at the pit but not by many of the other people of the village. Most of my experiences of the strike were not really in the village but in the pit yards and power stations across the north and Midlands. Trips to the village during the strike took place well before any sane people got out of bed. Soup kitchens and other local activities were done in the main by others.

A regular group of striking miners was involved in providing pensioners with coal. The Home Coal Society with help from the NUM Branch sorted this out. The coal had to be 'hand-picked' from sources on the pit top and delivered by the Home Coal lorry. It was a big commitment but was maintained until the first scab went in, then the NCB made every effort to exclude strikers from pit property, including the tips.

Coal picking to provide for my family was not on my agenda. I had a smokeless fuel fire but was not reliant on it. The pensioner coal suppliers were organised and needed no help from me. Helping out mates was a bit different. I found myself on railway cuttings working thin seams of coal with a pick and shovel. With a bit of organisation, it was possible to fill half a dozen big bags in a couple of hours. Coal picking during strikes had been a custom and practice in the industry for generations.

As the autumn of the strike arrived, more and more people descended onto pit tips to riddle coal from the waste. At my pit one young man, not a miner, was buried and suffocated. He became yet another fatality of the strike.

Where a live police operation existed at collieries, scavenging for fuel was pretty tricky. If a pit had any 'working miners' then management and police came down heavy. Dozens of miners found themselves arrested and dismissed for coal picking.

As the strike turned from weeks to months, I played my part collecting money and raising support through other trade union branches in Sheffield and Rotherham. Steel workers from South Yorkshire regularly donated cash collected at their workplace. Labour Party constituencies and university trade union branches adopted our pit and provided support in cash and kind.

As the weeks dragged on the value and contribution of Women Against Pit Closures increased. The pickets might have been shell-shocked but the women just kept on going.

More could have been done perhaps, but sustaining the strike was only part of the picture. *Winning* the strike proved to be the harder part. Picketing was time consuming and tiring. There were not enough hours in the day to do everything needed. Picketing became a ritual, and often a useless one at that, but it was the activity that got in the news, that kept the police and government awake at night. There seemed no other option.

Families who claimed social security was perhaps a bigger issue than food parcels and self-help. It was possible to claim for a few things for the families of strikers but not the strikers themselves. The Thatcher government had made sure strikers had no financial assistance from the state whatsoever, starving or not. This had not been the case on the 1972 and 1974 miners' strikes.

Local council social services were potentially very helpful. Unfortunately, the leader of Rotherham Council was not well disposed to the strike. He was a former NUM official himself but one of the right-wingers that had held sway in Yorkshire for many years before Scargill was elected first President of Yorkshire and then the National Union.

The man had previously railed against Rotherham teachers who had gone on strike demanding smaller class sizes. Now you would have thought any progressive person should try to improve the educational opportunities for working class kids; not this bloke. He considered teachers work-shy and suggested a shift down the pit might give them some idea about what hard work was really like.

More than anything, the council leader wanted to take Scargill down a peg or two. This was a common desire of some trade union and Labour leaders at the time, not just the Tories. Defeating 'Scargillism' was high on their agenda – obliterating mining communities was just collateral damage. The council leader was not in the mood to be helpful. Fortunately, other people were very helpful, including the constituency office of a local Labour MP.

A senior social worker I had met at one of the many meetings around the strike provided much of the information and support needed to make successful claims for dependents. And so the blockage from the leader of Rotherham Council was removed on this matter. There was no knowing what else he had done to undermine the strike.

The same councillor claimed he was never obstructive. But then, he also made other claims when embroiled in a scandal about missing money from a Miners' Welfare Club.

In August of the strike, I joined a delegation to Northern Ireland travelling via Stranraer and Larne. The trip was timed to coincide with the annual anti-internment events. A group of us from Yorkshire mining areas stayed with families in Ardoyne in North Belfast. A couple of the young miners joined the local youths one night battling with the RUC. I gave them a bollocking, but really had no control over them. They were lads from the Doncaster area and I was well used to their high spirits, yearning for action and downright stupidity. A quietly spoken local man had a word with them the next day. He was more than likely a Provo – they behaved themselves after that.

It wasn't a money-raising trip – you could hardly claim to be a deserving case in a place where a real war was going on. My lasting memory is being crouched behind a little wall in Andersonstown during a demonstration as plastic bullets filled the air. Alongside me amongst the cowering people was the wife of a striking miner who was also on the delegation.

We, and the rest of the delegation, escaped injury, but one young man was killed – shot in the chest at close range with a plastic bullet by the security forces. He was from the Republican community, unarmed and not a member of any paramilitary group.

The following is an extract from *Relatives for Justice*, dated 25th November, 2004:

The death of John Sean Downes – Former RUC officer's "Deep Shame".

Yesterday's Irish News reported that a former RUC officer who was on duty the day John Downes was killed by a plastic bullet in West Belfast has lambasted the police operation.

Edmund Gregory is highly critical of his superiors' decision to baton charge a Republican demonstration in an attempt to arrest US-based fundraiser Martin Galvin who was banned from the north.

John Downes was killed when he was struck in the chest at point-blank range by a plastic bullet in Andersonstown in the ensuing riot in August 1984.

In his memoir, 'Not Waving but Drowning', Mr Gregory describes the police actions as "stupid" and said the death left him feeling "deep shame".

Writing about the killing of Mr Downes, Mr Gregory describes the moment that a police snatch squad moved in:

"All hell broke loose. This was one of the most stupid operations I have ever seen in all my time as a policeman and one that I am not afraid to say filled me with deep shame."

Mr Gregory told the Irish News: "They (the Downes family) have my heartfelt sympathy. It was a peaceful parade. The crowd were in no way threatening."

A RUC officer was later acquitted of killing Mr Downes.

Experiences during the strike had hardened me to street battles with out-of-control security forces, but this was different. The police in the coalfields, thankfully, were not issued with baton rounds, otherwise they would no doubt have eagerly used them.

Delegation Visit to Belfast, early 1980s

It was November 1984 – an old friend from Italy got in touch. He was the equivalent of a local councillor in a small town in the hills south of Bologna.

The strike was big news in Italy; a labour movement used to bitter struggles and political clashes of all sorts could not quite get their heads around a strike that went on for nearly a year. But the Communist Party in Emilia Romagna wanted to help. Communism was not a dirty word in this part of Italy where the Partisans took on the occupying German army well before the Brits and Yanks turned up. Over 700 local people had been executed by the Waffen SS in retribution for partisan activity.

The invite to Bologna came from young activists from the local Communist Party (PCI) and they asked me to do a speaking tour over a period of about ten days.[49]

This meant meeting senior local politicians and trade union leaders who had given their blessing but I was left in the charming company of a burly, chain-smoking guy in a KGB-style coat. It soon became obvious no one said *no* to this bloke or questioned him in any way – a Communist Party organiser straight out of politburo central casting. Thankfully, he warmed a little after some pasta and fine red wine.

My name (wrongly spelt) was on posters in the corridors of Bologna University and on the gates of engineering factories. Workers downed tools and marched to the gates to hear me speak – the minder saw to that. Students crowded into lecture theatres. One of the venues was a basketball stadium. Some 5,000 basketball fans had to listen to me bang on about the miners' strike before the match could start! My Italian was pretty feeble so my old mate did the translation. Speeches were kept short – there is nothing worse than long drawn-out speeches and the subsequent translation; it kills any impact.

Towards the end of the trip a huge cheque was presented – lira always seems to come in millions and it wasn't easy to grasp how much it was really worth. The total appeared to be over 18,000,000 lira. It was particularly pleasing that the Ducati motorbike workers raised 500,000 lira.

In January 1985 I received a letter from the 'minder' in Bologna:

I want to wish you and your family a Happy New Year and hope that 1985 will be the year of victory for British miners and the N.U.M.

---

49 Jonathan Saunders: *Across Frontiers, International Support for the Miners' Strike* 1984/5.

I want to thank you for the opportunity that you gave us, the people and workers of Bologna, to fully realise the contents of the glorious struggle of British miners. Our Union Area Office, that was given the target of 4,000,000 lira, has up to date collected 13,600,000 lira (£5,500 approx.), and we think we can collect another 3 or 4 million lira in the next few days. The total sum collected for striking miners in the Bologna area is now 30,000,000 lira (£12,000).

This letter is also to inform you that on Monday, Jan. 7, two young metal workers, fond of photography, will come to you, as Marcello already told you. They want to take a lot of pictures of the miners' lives and their present strike, and then sell them to magazines, agencies etc. hoping in this way to help the miners' cause.

I hope you can help them in doing this. Hoping that this too can represent a small contribution to the miners' fight and the fight of all workers against the Thatcherites and monetarists in Europe.

Hoping to see you soon, maybe in Sheffield, I wish you all the best.

(Bologna Area Union Office)

P.S. all the best from Marcello

The money was sent through official channels, but I couldn't help think we could have made better use of it back at my own pit.

The two Italian photographers met up with me and I took them on a tour of various picketing hotspots in Yorkshire. They were not entirely enamoured by 4am starts. The young photographers also wrote back in April 1985:

We are not able to write English very well and for this reason we are so 'short' as you can see.

We are sending to you some images that we have done during our permanence in Yorkshire in January 85.

Thank you very much for your wonderful collaboration and hospitality; we are sorry for the Miners' Strike that is finished.

Good luck to you and good future for the N.U.M.

The level of international interest in the strike and the support of international trades unions were unprecedented. The Tory press liked to cook up stories of 'Moscow Gold' and the NUM and other trade unions were routinely linked with the USSR and therefore in the pay of the Kremlin. The brutal truth was that Poland (amongst other countries), a (supposedly) communist satellite of the Soviet Union at the time, continued to export coal to the UK during the strike.

A cold Christmas with no end to the strike in sight arrived. But it turned out to be a high point. The material support for the strike in terms of food was at its highest. Sheffield Trades Council, to name but one example, had a voucher for a large food parcel with a Christmas dinner for all the 2,000-plus miners that lived within the city boundaries. Food convoys came in from around the country. The miners' welfares were decked with food parcels, and Xmas presents for hundreds of kids.

A monumental effort had been made from supporters across the UK and the rest of the world. Sometimes you had to just stop and think. All this was done without any formal organisation – no Oxfam, no Save the Children Fund, no Children in Need, no United Nations and in the teeth of opposition from the British state.

There was standing room only in the Welfare as Father Christmas did his bit. The hit tune of that time was *Do they Know It's Christmas* by Band Aid, a song about third world hunger. *Feed the World* was soon changed to *Feed the Miners* and sung raucously by lads with a few pints down them.

The experience of that Christmas was priceless and reveals the best about the human spirit. Yet the vultures were circling and time was not on our side.

I had few memories of Christmases down the years. Nothing really registered.

Odd fragments from when I was a kid sometimes popped up. A Christmas party at the Co-op, carol singing to try and blag a bit of money out of the neighbours. Yet this Christmas stands out and is certainly one I remember fondly. Fond memories often lose out to the memories of bad times and sadness. Maybe I simply couldn't remember the good times.

As the strike dragged on, my brother and I helped set up a network of active strikers. We wanted to try to break out of the daily rut, bring in new tactics and hopefully make some progress where picketing clearly wasn't effective. As it turned out, it was too late to really have any impact on the outcome of the strike, but something needed to be done to at least try.

This network called itself Yorkshire Miners Campaign Group 85. An ad hoc national network existed and convened itself on a couple of occasions with the help of senior academics in Durham and South Wales. There were plenty of ideas and analysis, but no way of steering activity in the strike. The NUM leadership were riding a tiger they dearly wanted to get off, but how? The default position was to plough on in the same furrow, stuck in that 1972 time warp.

I personally have no recollection of the NUM making approaches directly to workers in other industries. If they did, it was at senior level and with limited success. After all, the steel union leadership had betrayed the strike and other trade unions, such as Frank Chapple's electricians, openly opposed the strike and ridiculed Scargill.

The Yorkshire Miners' Campaign Group 85 produced several leaflets in the last few months of the strike trying to appeal to other trade unions and the public. We presented arguments for a progressive energy policy. Whatever happened at the end of the strike, there needed to be an agenda in the public domain that supported the coal industry. There was a national economic and environmental case that never saw the light of day because of the constant attention to aggro, division and bitterness. Yes, the strike was about communities and jobs, but everyone had a stake in the future energy policy of the UK and for that matter, the rest of the world.

The introduction of new technology in the coal mines was hit and miss – after all, computers and the like were yet to be deployed in many industries, let alone in everyday life. The advent of the Mine Operating System (MINOS)[50] had many threats but also some opportunities. The Campaign Group pressed the NUM to tackle the issue head on and try to harness new technology for the good of the workers, not just the profit bottom line. A shorter working week beckoned but of course the NCB was more interested in cutting jobs. The privatised industry would eventually reap the rewards.

The Group sometimes met at Northern College in a country mansion of a former coal owner to the west of Barnsley. This was a further education college that focused on adult learning amongst working class communities. Speakers and participants from the labour movement and academia were invited and it was a welcome relief from police harassment.

One of the senior staff at the college at that time was Mo Mowlam, later to become an MP and Minister in the Blair Government. She was welcoming and chatty but some while later, she was to remark that me and my brother were the "two most dangerous Trotskyites in Yorkshire." A wry smile comes to my face whenever I recall this comment. Neither of us were in any way dangerous and had most definitely never been Trotskyites. I didn't mind backhanded compliments but 'dangerous' – to whom? More annoying was being labelled a Trotskyite. Clearly Mo was better briefed when she later took over the job leading the Northern Ireland peace process.

The Yorkshire Miners Campaign Group 85 – known by some as the 'Sunshine Miners' because of the sun emblem on our lapel badge – was one of the networks that carried on some years after the strike. It worked with officers in the NUM national office, academics and some MPs. Its main focus continued to be energy policy, new technology and investment in the coal mines as well as clean coal technology for the power sector. Needless to say, as the years rolled by, the pits shut. Successive governments failed to come up with any coherent energy policy other than privatisation. The Group's words had fallen on deaf ears.

---

50 MINOS. Mine Operating System – a broad package of computer-controlled systems to run coal mines. Introduced piecemeal during the 1980s and 90s.

Sifting through drawers stuffed with old papers going back to the strike and other events relating to the final years of the coal industry, I was surprised just how pessimistic and frustrated I must have been. Re-reading my own words over thirty years later, they appeared unnecessarily strident. But that was how I felt at the time.

My frustrations with the conduct of the miners' strike were subject to a great deal of self-censorship. I did not want to decry what is universally thought to be an epic period in British trade union history. It was heroic and it was way beyond the call of duty. Examples of sacrifice and solidarity on the one side; betrayal and assault by the state on the other.

So as the years passed a positive spin was put on the year-long battle and most of us went along with that. We were loyal and proud members of the NUM.

But surely nobody really believes that the miners won – do they?

An illustration of such frustrations can be found in the transcription of an interview I did on 14 October 1984 at a time when national negotiations appeared to be making some progress – but as we now know, not for long.

Everybody's undergone a lot of hardship and made a lot of sacrifices, some more than others: some people are in nick, some are dead. But I don't really think we are really yet in a position to win this strike in the way we want to. Because I don't think that when we went into the strike back in March we really had a strategy of how to win it.

The union was still, to some extent, relying on the organisational memories left over from 1972 and 1974 on how you actually go about winning a coal strike. But there were a couple of things that completely changed this picture:

- *The use of the police and the whole state apparatus;*

- *The Government reorganised power generation in this country over the past seven months: increasing oil burn, converting coal fired power stations, building up the nuclear output – so we've never been clear how or when our economic stranglehold upon the country would become apparent.*

The vast majority of activists have been deployed in military style actions with the police and I don't think we have stopped a cobble of coal through picketing during this strike. The rail and seamen's unions have stopped it for us and there's never been a serious attempt to go beyond that. And it took so long, maybe we've had to earn the solidarity from other workers – by being out so long they felt bad about it.

The use of the police has coloured the strike and forced us into actions we hadn't previously conceived of where the role of picketing has become just one battle with the police rather than an attempt to stop the movement of coal or to stop scabs going in. The police put themselves between us and the objectives so of course, first of all you've got to take them on. The NUM is not capable of taking on the police in that way. That has been a real drain on the resources we've got.

Talking to people at a local level would have been more effective. We spend a lot of time involved in flying picketing and that time could have been spent in flying delegations, in actually getting to the factory gates, in talking to convenors, get a meeting called, present your case and then see what happens, much more direct links that way.

An Oral History[51] written and published not long after the strike, also finds me ruminating on what might have been and missed opportunities:

I think imagination is something we were definitely lacking. The government had planned to win the strike in a very sophisticated and a very hard way and we had not planned to do the same. In 1984 the TUC is in a shambles and there's four million unemployed. …We can't do it on our own and we should have made a lot more effort building alliances with members of other unions, in the communities, in the Labour Party and wherever you can build an alliance.

Reflecting once more, I considered the concerns written at the time and recorded by others just after the strike, were justified as well as genuine. I was

---

51 *Thurcroft. A Village and the Miners' Strike*, Gibbon and Steyne. 1986.

a NUM activist trying to win the strike. There is always a tendency to look at events, close ranks and stick with the orthodox version. But different actions could have been taken and were possible at the time, not just in hindsight. These views were in no way complaints or defeatism, but part of an attempt to win the strike and not just go down in a blaze of glory. If what you are doing is not working, try something else! Women Against Pit Closures were campaigning creatively, but we were too slow to spot it at the time.

Whilst some of strike activists were trying to influence the agenda and tactics of the strike, some workmates came up with an entirely different approach. I woke one morning to be told that the Administration Block at the pit had been demolished.

Demolished? How? Well, it's fairly easy with a 10 tonnes bulldozer. Someone, or some people, had hijacked the bulldozer. It was usually used on the pit tip. They then calmly flattened the administration block overnight. The demolition was widely reported in the press and on television and it served to drive home in public consciousness just how desperate things were becoming. Lashing out at the NCB in this way somehow seemed excusable.

What was never excusable was the manslaughter of a taxi driver in South Wales in November of the strike. Two 21-year-old strikers had dropped a concrete block on the taxi from a road bridge – killing the driver who was taking a scab to work. The two young men were charged with murder and given life sentences. It was later changed on appeal to manslaughter and they did five years in jail. The strength of feeling was so high, bad things were going to happen. Those of us embroiled in picketing and police harassment were always acutely aware of how it was so easy to let things get out of hand with tragedy waiting in the wings.

Throughout the strike the activities, moods and expectations in the coalfield areas were punctuated by a tortuous cycle of national events. This involved talks that were on – then just as quickly off again. Dockers were coming out on all-out strike in July to stop coal imports – then they didn't. Tough talking from some of the better trade union leaders but little action. It was mainly the rail unions who gave direct support by not moving coal.

Bizarre events such as the connection between the NUM national office and Colonel Gaddafi served to confuse and annoy the strikers and feed press frenzy. What was Roger Windsor, the Chief Executive of the NUM national office, doing in Libya? It provided those with an anti-strike view with all the evidence they needed that Scargill was an enemy of the state. No one to this day really knows who Roger Windsor was working for. Stories emerged years later about his murky connections, but nothing definite was proved. He certainly was not working to support the strike.

It is easy to assume some hidden malign hands were at work. Undercover operations, stings, 'agent provocateurs' were all plausible explanations but there was no damning evidence. These things can be dismissed as stupid – but who was pulling whose strings? Undercover operations were far more prevalent than anyone thought at the time. Policemen subsequently were found to have gone so far undercover they had kids with the women they were spying on. By 2022 the 'spy cop' stories made it to primetime television – the drama series *Sherwood* gave the telly-watching public a good insight.

The financial position of the union was dire and little understood by the public. Civil actions became a key weapon of the government after the summer of 1984. The strike was ruled illegal under Tory anti-trade union law in September. The NUM was then fined £200,000 for being in contempt of court with the members of the NUM National Executive made liable for the fine. All NUM assets were then frozen by sequestration (also under the same Tory law) – an action unprecedented outside a dictatorship. This was a massive issue that is so easy to forget and which no amount of picketing could address. All the important activities were out of the rank-and-file control, played out on the national stage with the government holding all the cards. It became harder and harder to stay positive.

The ongoing negotiations between the NUM and NCB under ACAS (Advisory, Conciliation and Arbitration Service) were punctuated with legal action designed to crush the NUM. The shadowy figures near the Tory

Government pulled many of the strings. This type of legal assault on the trade unions transformed the UK into the Thatcher and post-Thatcher world we have all now got so used to over the last few decades. It was a seismic shift in the power relationships between trade unions, employers and government.

Unconventional actions were taken to keep hold of NUM funds. It may seem cloak and dagger, but what was the alternative? Sometimes it seemed farcical, but it's not easy to distinguish between fact and fiction as events unfolded at breakneck speed. There were plenty of rumours and many opportunities for dirty tricks from government. Some day we may find out more.

Inevitably, everything became difficult and open to criticism from detractors and supporters alike. Money had to disappear. Dealings with Polish bank accounts and alleged carrier bags full of cash fed the right-wing press. More smoke and mirrors. Still, after much media speculation over many years, the truth is largely unknown. Many questions remain unanswered and many more questions weren't even asked.

There was widespread support from local Labour parties but not the leadership. Neil Kinnock's campaign against the left in the Labour Party included giving no succour to Scargill. Kinnock paid lip service to the striking miners in South Wales, but gave no help or encouragement to the strike elsewhere. A defeat of the miners seemed likely and he had no desire to associate himself with the consequences. Scargill needed to be discredited above all else.

When Labour finally got into power in 1997 in the new Blair era, there was palpable relief on new government ministers' faces that the NUM had been defeated by Thatcher and was no longer strong enough to cause them any more trouble. The NUM and coal mining were now the stuff of nostalgia, gone was the ever-present threat governments had feared for so long. The potential economic and political power of the NUM was tamed at last. The leaders of all the main political parties quietly celebrated.

The biggest rollercoaster ride for the striking miners was the disappointing outcome from their colleagues in the pit deputies' union, NACODS[52]. They held a ballot for strike action with 82% voting in favour. They used this bargaining chip in long drawn-out talks with the NCB instead of coming out

---

52 National Association of Colliery Overmen, Deputies and Shotfirers.

and shortening the strike by months. A victory was possible for the miners, but the government didn't want to hand it to Scargill and the rest of the so-called 'enemy within.'

The NACODS leadership did not use the power invested by their members very well. They negotiated a Modified Colliery Review Procedure, which gave the unions the option to talk to the NCB about individual pit closures. It was a toothless procedure that was used later merely to divert any fight against pit closures down a blind alley. Not one of the pits that subsequently closed successfully made use of the procedure. It was like Chamberlain holding up his useless piece of paper from Herr Hitler.

Most striking miners were incensed – what a chance to win the strike! 82% for strike action and then no strike and no support! Others on strike took it as a cue to concede defeat and contemplate the unthinkable: going back to work past their striking mates. Each time hopes were lifted and then dashed a few more waverers slipped back into work in the dead of night.

Another morning, another hapless shuffle around the bedroom to try to make sense of the surroundings. A shattered dream whirling in pieces around in my mind. I slowly get a picture of the here and now. A light might help … yes that's a bit better as familiar shapes come into view.

Dressed, coffee, car keys and away. Except it's not morning and I'm not going to work. It's the middle of the night and I have to be at the Welfare before 4am if possible. Oh, it's possible all right, but probably fucking pointless. This is a 'new' old car. It's roadworthy, but only just. Thankfully, it's still got six months' MOT. There is a disturbing view of the road under the front passenger door waiting to be filled with resin. Well at least it started, after about three turns of the key – not bad for winter. The Welfare, and I enter the side door with a dim light in front. A very big teapot is in use.

Cold and dark with the odd glisten of frost and dismal street lighting, we left the hall after a cup of tea. There was always plenty of tea to be had in this strike. Tea and sympathy were fine, soup kitchens even better. All well and good, a bit of comfort. It wouldn't last – the 'bad guys' were out there trying to do you in.

Keeping off the main road we walked up a back street. Those dark winter mornings were all cloak and dagger, wandering and wondering what lay around the next corner.

A convoy of Range Rovers turned right onto the back street, dimly lit. 'Belfast' cow catches[53] easily identifying them as the South Yorkshire police 'hit squad'. Still well before dawn and icy underfoot we four pickets kept walking trying to make out all was normal.

"Now then, you fuckers, what are you up to?" bellowed the top brass officer, the buttons and braid on his uniform twinkling in the street light. He marched alone towards the target of his anger with all the swagger of a middle-aged bloke trying, and failing, to prove his masculinity.

Silly me couldn't resist opening my mouth:

"Walking through the village … no law against walking through the village is there?" Instantly I realised the mistake.

"Well, we have one here, don't we … a fucking communist. You, sunshine, have too much of what the cat licks its arse with," the police officer kindly informed everyone at full volume.

Squaring up to me in the gloom the officer began to relish his power: "Come on then have a fucking go, yer little shit! Come on! Come on!"

My temper rose but I glanced around. We were surrounded by twenty police, which were poor odds. Not another murmur. We moved on up the street as the gathered police stood in silence not wanting to spoil any of the fun their senior officer was having.

"Now fuck off before we knock you into next week," was all the officer had to offer now. His chance of a scrap seemed to have subsided.

The same senior officer with an attitude problem got his face into national media earlier in the strike by arresting Arthur Scargill. In 1989, he was at Hillsborough football ground, watching Liverpool fans die in front of him and his fellow officers. An 'urban myth' about him still does the rounds: he once drove his Range Rover into a concrete bollard disguised as a snowman in the winter of the strike. Anybody in South Yorkshire who does not now know his name has not been paying attention.

---

53 A skirt on the front of the Range Rover, designed to stop objects from going under it.

We four, hands stuffed deep into pockets, walked towards the pit lane. It's usually safer on the pit lane. On the pit lane you are on a picket line; anywhere else in the village at this early hour you are a potential criminal. You may be attempting to intimidate scabs, risking arrest under long forgotten laws.

An old dirty green single-decker bus chugs down the pit lane. Just to add to the farce it's got the destination 'Glasgow' on the front. Wire mesh covers all its windows and shadowy individuals can just be seen inside but are not identifiable. Who they are and how many is something known only to themselves, the NCB management and the police.

Standing with a couple of dozen pickets, a handful of police try to put on their best 'friends of the community' appearance. Not for them the effing and blinding, truncheon-wielding, shield-carrying antics of their colleagues. They too like their creature comforts and standing about on a dark winter morning isn't one of them. The overtime pay comes in handy, but they too are getting a bit sick of the routine.

The bus passes and enters the pit yard with little fuss. It's ten months into the strike and the strikers know they are wasting their breath shouting any more insults. Now with hands shoved even deeper into pockets, we pickets shuffle from one foot to the other to try to warm up our feet. The light strengthens from the east.

It had all been very different ten months ago … ten months and still two more to go? Looking back, it is hard to take in just how long that strike lasted. A lifetime of experiences crammed into one year.

Much has been written about the talks and machinations that brought the strike to an end[54]. The complex relationships of Thatcher, her ministers, and MacGregor on one side and Scargill, his NUM colleagues and the TUC on the other side, served to blur fact and fiction.

The Special Delegate Conference of March 1985 was a torturous affair. Interpretations differ, but one version of the conference and NUM National

---

54 Beckett and Henke: *Marching to the Faultlines*, 2009.

Executive Committee (NEC) machinations rings true.[55] Arthur Scargill ruled that the NEC was bound by the last decision of Conference to stay out on strike. The Conference was incensed that the NEC were abdicating the responsibility to take a lead. The NEC was told to re-convene, but they still could not make a decision and reported a 'failure to agree' to the Special Conference. Eventually a vote was taken and by 98 to 91 the NUM decided on a return to work with no settlement.

So ended one of the most painful days in the history of the British trades' union movement.[56]

No one wanted to put his name to the potential calamity. Arthur for one was adamant nobody could put the blame on him. Had the lions been led by donkeys? Who were the donkeys and who were the lions? 'Failure is an orphan' as they say. Some focused on the history books, but others had to make the best of it for everybody's sake.

There were mixed messages from the NUM leadership for some time. It was irritating and disheartening when, early in the new year of 1985, Peter Heathfield, the General Secretary of the NUM, made a public statement that the power stations had enough coal supplies to go on for several more months. Arthur Scargill had confidently told his members early in the strike that there would be power cuts within eight or nine weeks.

The NUM had been criticised by fellow trade unionists for going on strike in spring with months of warmer weather ahead. Having stuck it out through the winter of 84/5 surely it was just a matter of time. We had waited for 'General Winter' to arrive and put economic pressure on the government, but it was an illusion. It appeared the NUM leadership itself had given in or at least had no more to offer its battle-weary troops.

I had a lot of time and respect for Peter Heathfield but I did not want to hear what he had to say. "Why on earth did the General Secretary make that

---

[55] Hilary Cave, *NUM Special Delegate Conferences 83–85* in Nottinghamshire and Derbyshire Labour History Society Newsletter, September 2020.

[56] Hilary Cave, *NUM Special Delegate Conferences 83–85* in Nottinghamshire and Derbyshire Labour History Society Newsletter, September 2020.

public statement? How can we stop a return to work if our leaders are being so pessimistic? What were we supposed to do, Peter, stop out for another fucking year?" I asked myself over and over again, but never openly criticised him, or indeed any of the NUM leadership.

Hundreds had been sacked during the strike. Their fate lay in the balance. Many strikers were incensed, especially in Kent where the area NCB had sacked first and asked questions later.

At my own pit dozens had been sacked. Amongst them were twelve young miners in the village arrested one night for a host of charges including besetting. This was a charge going back to the 19th century. Legal definitions seem to differ, but it more or less means:

'Conduct by someone that causes another person to feel hemmed in or a person to feel surrounded, for a person to feel attacked on all sides.'

George Nash, a boot-fitter, surrendered his bail, and was charged on remand with having unlawfully watched and beset certain premises, with other persons, with a view to intimidate certain workpeople from doing an act which they had a legal right to do.[57]

It was one of the anti-trade union laws of its time.

The background to these sackings stemmed from resentment towards a small number of men in the village who worked as contractors in the mines over the border in Nottinghamshire. As the strike wore on this became unacceptable to the local strikers. One of the contractors fancied himself as a bit of a hard case and was fond of telling people how much money he was earning whilst they were on strike.

After a social evening in the village run by a Sheffield Labour Party constituency, some lads gathered at the house of the contractor. Songs were sung and a window broken. The strike breaker let fly with a twelve-bore shotgun and things got a bit heated.

The day after, a number of people were arrested and twelve eventually

---

57 *Standard, 1881* 28 October, page 2.

charged. The guy firing the shotgun was excused his behaviour. The twelve young men were sacked by the NCB. To this day it remains a puzzle how the arrests could have been made several hours after the incident. Why these twelve lads? Who had provided any evidence?

This type of incident was common across the coalfields. Three men were sacked from another South Yorkshire pit whilst standing in their own gardens. They were unfortunate to have a scab living near them.

The sackings and victimisation were something the Coal Board boasted about. The Chairman MacGregor was on record as saying the miners will:

"Have to pay the price for insubordination and insurrection, and boy we are going to make it stick!"

Once again, the oppressors unwittingly reveal their true nature:

Insubordination – defiance of authority, refusal to obey orders.

Insurrection – violent action taken by a large group of people against the rulers of their country in order to remove them from office.[58]

So now we know. Now we get the picture. That's what happens when you try to defend your jobs and communities.

Some years later I yet again I found myself browsing through old leaflets, NCB letters and strike memorabilia and there are some things difficult to grasp. One is the desperation as the strike begins to fold. Leaflets put out by the Yorkshire Miners' Campaign Group highlight low coal stocks at power stations and the loss of a unit at Ferrybridge C power station. Where the NCB and Government could, they were moving coal. At our pit, unwashed coal on the stack was being taken by scab lorries to power stations. They must have needed it. But it was too late.

A leaflet from the Campaign Group urged on 1 February 1985:
'Stand together, Victory will come!' Then on 23 February it is reported in

---

58 Dictionary definitions.

another leaflet that some miners, having returned to work, are so sickened they came back out on strike.

It doesn't wear off – you feel as guilty as hell!

Later still on 1st March, it is pointed out in another leaflet that the NCB/Government refusal to negotiate a settlement is in breach of the Coal Industry Nationalisation Act (1946). NCB top management are no more than Tory Government puppets. Miners are exhorted to 'Stay on Strike!' The same leaflet puts 196,000 still on strike and 46,000 miners who never went on strike, leaving a drift back of some 28,000 miners. In Yorkshire, of the 56,000 workforce, only 8,000 were back on 26 February 1985.

Returning to work without addressing the issue of sackings and victimisation seemed a betrayal. Options to re-ignite the strike flickered, but only briefly. Realism weighed heavy, even on the most die-hard strikers.

I had kept it all together for over a year. As I read in the morning paper on a March morning in 1985 that the strike was over, a year after it started, I filled up and quietly cried at the kitchen table. I left the kitchen and sat in my room – I could not face conversations or explanations. I will not have been the only one crushed and speechless.

Hollow inside, hoping and despairing in the self-same moment. Nothing left in the tank – not for a while at least anyway.

There was so much unfinished business that was briefly swept under the carpet only to re-emerge as the pits began to close with little opposition.

Fearing to hope and fearing the worst, the striking miners and their families stepped into the unknown: the new normal.

Cortonwood – late 1984 . Acrylic on canvas. © David J Parry.

10
RETURNING TO WORK AND REBUILDING THE NUM BRANCH

A return to work after a year on strike with no settlement seemed implausible – for some, unthinkable – but that is what happened. I did not like it one bit, but at least we could earn some money and take a break from police harassment.

A march back to work was organised at most pits.

Those pits with the majority of men who had broken the strike no doubt made no show of the end of the strike. A sigh of relief perhaps, but surely the strike breakers felt ashamed of themselves. Was this some kind of victory for them or did they too feel a sense of loss and defeat? What do they think ten, twenty or thirty years later looking back on the destruction of their communities and way of life? Certainly, some of the brave people in the Midlands coalfields that stuck it out faced a hard time and blatant victimisation. They were the outcasts.

Finding myself at a low ebb, I was inclined not to care about how these people managed to live with themselves. But deep down I couldn't help but wonder how to handle these deep divisions. How to reach across divides? What can be done to make the fight for communities actually mean something in practice rather than just trip off the tongue of a speaker at a rally?

The march back at Thurcroft was a proud affair with banners held high. The local Women Against Pit Closures group turned out in force having found a role and a voice that was now listened to. It was heart-warming stuff, but it was mostly a big relief that some kind of normality had returned. We (those marching down the pit lane) had all stayed loyal and could hold our heads high whilst many others could not. There was some tension in the air as the loyal strikers would soon have to face and mix with the dreaded scabs. But not on the day of the march back as it turned out.

We marched from the Welfare to the pit yard next to the management office block. Hundreds of people, miners and others, stood around in the pit yard with the pit banner, not sure what to do next. Being back on NCB property felt a little odd. Some wandered over to where the administration offices used to be – now mysteriously demolished.

It was a reunion after twelve months for some. There was some catching up with each other and general blather. Relief was etched in the smiles and laughter and exchange of tales. Retribution and pay back were not on the agenda.

An old collier, who had no intention of working, turned up in his pin-striped, three-piece suit. His nickname was Slope and, with a full beard and long hair, he looked straight out of a country and western band – apart from the suit. He had only days to work and he would retire with a redundancy package, as would many others. At least he stuck it out and could bow out with honour.

As an NUM Committee member since 1982, I was updated by the NUM branch officials on what management expected. However, there was not much chance of getting any useful work out of the assembled miners so the real return to work was put off until 6am the next day. The crowd mostly wandered off back down the pit lane to the club, the house, the allotment or the pigeon lofts.

The following day people were deployed as normal and, in many ways, they just picked up where they left off. Despite all the scare stories from the NCB, this pit had survived the year with no major geological problems.

The pit had seen dozens of men break the strike but it was never really clear just how many. A rough estimate of about thirty per cent had gone back. The vast majority of those had returned in the last month when any hope of victory had run out.

At our pit scabs were graded: those in the BBC (Back Before Christmas) category were shunned. Later returners were afforded a bit more understanding. But they knew who they were, what they had done and who they had let down. This was not the case in other pits where only a handful may have broken the strike. In such pits there was no understanding, no olive branch, only endless rejection.

It was a bit of a mystery what the NCB had been up to in the last couple of months of the strike. Management at senior level, backed up by the Board and government, had systematically targeted individuals and either bribed or threatened them. Few miners who returned to work just woke up one morning and walked in.

For the older age group, the promise of a big redundancy payment was the clincher, but for younger men, just what was the incentive or threat apart from earning a wage for the first time in months? The secret meetings with potential scabs, the cloak and dagger goings on – what exactly happened and who said what to whom remain largely unknown to the strikers and the scabs aren't telling.

It is difficult to judge but much of the pressure and support to stay loyal came more directly from Women Against Pit Closures. Where the women did not organise for whatever reason, the support and pressure were absent. Being part of something bigger, something collective, kept people going. If you kept yourself to yourself, you were vulnerable to doubt, government propaganda and NCB bribes.

When it came to the official union-backed return to work, more rumours did the rounds. Armthorpe, near Doncaster, was back out on strike. I knew many of the Armthorpe crew well, they had shared many a barricade with us and it came as no surprise – they were up for World War Three if needs be.

As it turned out, they did not picket other pits and they too returned to work, if a little later than the rest of South Yorkshire.

Prior to the return to work, each employee at the pit received a short letter from the manager. Here is the full text:

Dear Sir,

Now that the strike is over, I am sending this letter to each man at the Colliery. To those returning to work for the first time, I extend a warm welcome.

Everybody's first concern must be to work safely and to avoid accidents. Those of you who have not been at work for twelve months will take some time to recover your "pit legs", and you will need a while to re-acclimatise yourself. My management staff and officials will be working more closely than usual with you in the early days to see that we all return quickly to proper safety methods.

The normal systems of deployment will be used from the start. We are all going to have to work together. Personal feelings must not stand in the way of getting the job done safely and effectively.

Firm but fair discipline will be imposed as it always has been. Violence of whatever form, including fighting, physical provocation and verbal abuse or intimidation, will be considered an act of gross misconduct carrying the usual penalty. All men will be treated equally. Instructions from management or officials must be carried out.

We have a big job to do to regain the confidence of our customers on whom all our futures depend.

I could not suppress a wry smile on noticing the manager had been recently converted to the Marxist principle: '*All men be treated equally.*' He was yet to wake up to the fact that women also worked at the pit. Some of the canteen women were the most active in Women Against Pit Closures.

For my part, I started again on the afternoon shift. All dressed up in clean orange pit gear, the newly returned men stood about before crossing the pit yard to the shaft.

"Where do the good guys stand?", I shouted to the twenty odd men dressed for mining for the first time in over a year outside the pit head baths.

Not sure if any of these blokes had returned to work before the end of the strike, I glanced awkwardly around. Laughter and banter suggested they were all on the side of the angels. Scabs, I assumed, would sneak off and find somewhere out of the gaze of strikers. I was pretty sure I was with the good guys, at least for the time being.

And that was the difficulty. This pit had plenty of scabs; a minority yes, but how do you operate a pit with a divided workforce? How do you run a trade union with a divided workforce? Other pits faced this problem but many did not. They had stayed solid and getting rid of a couple of scabs was straightforward – transfer them or retire them – management wanted coal production, not more hassle. What could you do with dozens?

Having spent months despising such people I now, not only had to work with them, but I had to encourage their better selves and rebuild the creaking NUM branch.

I was not an NUM official but had been active in the branch since I started at the pit. Within a few weeks of returning to the coal face I had a message from the NUM branch treasurer, who was taking redundancy. He suggested I should stand for the job. Quickly on the heels of this approach from one branch official, the NUM branch delegate told me he too was taking redundancy. It was decided being delegate was more suitable. The job involved representing the NUM Branch at national and regional meetings as well as local negotiations with management.

Unopposed, I was elected NUM Delegate and was re-elected unopposed on two further occasions until the pit closed in 1992. I took this to mean the membership thought I was doing a good job. Or maybe I was kidding myself.

The main task was to re-establish the credibility of the NUM with all the workforce. The Branch had to therefore be effective at defending the interests of all the members. Thankfully, the core scabs had no interest in trade unionism; they believed that their own subservient behaviour with management would bring them all the rewards they sought.

The Branch Committee was made up of active strikers now and a new generation had taken the lead. We didn't feel defeated – not yet anyway.

Within weeks of settling down to normality and coal production the NUM Branch was informed a Tory Minister was planning to visit the colliery. The purpose of the visit was merely a publicity stunt to give the impression the Tories and miners were friends really, with a common purpose. The government thought it was a good gesture, a step towards burying the hatchet perhaps.

The NUM Branch was adamant they could not collude in such manipulation and an emergency meeting was called in the pit club. The options on the table were to walk out as soon as the Minister turned up or call a 24-hour strike timed for his visit. The meeting voted for a 24-hour strike – each miner losing a day's wage. The Minister, David Hunt, never showed up but had a rant in the local press:

The shadow of Scargillism still looms large over the future of this great industry, which has a bright future provided the militants are not allowed to wreck it.[59]

The rest of the publicity was about the strike and the solidarity of the workforce. Solidarity was now being rebuilt following the divisions towards the end of the year-long strike.

Another month went by, then another strike. This time it was far more important. The bloke who first broke the strike at Thurcroft pit went back in September 1984 on his own. He wasn't joined by anyone else for months. He'd previously worked in the developments on the same shift as me, so I knew him. I had even spoken to him over the summer at a local rally in Dinnington. I tried to reassure him that it was all worth it but he seemed at the end of his tether. The trouble was no one could really help – the help this guy needed was paying his huge mortgage.

As a UDM member no one wanted to work with him and he became a source of simmering aggravation at the pit. As a strike breaker he had been an asset to the powers-that-be. As a scab amongst loyal union people, he became a liability, an awkward diversion from coal production.

---

59 *Sheffield Morning Telegraph*, 28 August 1985.

None of us expected him to join the UDM and try to get others to do the same. It was a surprise because it was assumed he didn't have the bottle or motivation do anything but look after his own sorry arse. But then again, he had gone back into work – one man against everyone else. Who was pulling his strings? Was it his idea or had someone got to him?

Another branch meeting, again another vote, this time for an all-out strike if he was not moved. No one, not even those who had gone back before the end of the long 84/85 strike, wanted the pit to carry the stigma of the UDM. No one wanted all that shit raking up again.

Management caved in – this loner wasn't worth the trouble. The 'super-scab' was transferred to a pit in North Nottinghamshire and the UDM stayed put in the Midlands coalfields. The UDM were occasionally heard to complain when British Coal[60] shut their pits one by one. Their hopes of favourable treatment dashed.

In a chance meeting down a supermarket aisle, I came across the same bloke a year or so later. I was polite and reserved. I said hello, curious to try to understand what made the guy tick. He looked back straight into my eyes. I saw fear, shame and anger but we both stayed calm.

In an instant the bloke's wife came around the corner and spotted me. She launched into me with as much venom as she could muster:

"You lot, you ought to be ashamed of yourselves … just bullies the lot of yer! Look what you've done to him … he's dying of cancer and it's all your fault … your fault!"

There was no adequate response to this verbal assault and damning accusation. Dying of cancer? My fault?

I gave the husband a glance – perhaps he had something more to say, a word or two that might bridge the gaping hole between us. But there was no eye contact from him as his wife stood defiant. I slipped away in retreat from the angry woman. It was the last I saw or heard of the man. I for one cannot bear grudges for ever and I am always ready to forgive but can't really forget.

---

60 The National Coal Board became British Coal in 1987.

Successful disputes that stopped the rot were not the only good news in the months following the return to work. Our pit had twelve sacked miners to support. It was a source of constant regret that the return to work had not included an amnesty.

Some people may forget and most people never knew and it's only afterwards you start to count. During the strike 20,000 people were injured or hospitalised. Two miners were killed on the picket line and three died digging for coal. One taxi driver was killed by striking miners. Some 200 strikers spent time in prison. Over 900 were sacked and over 300 *never* got their jobs back.[61]

After some diligent work by area NUM officials and the legal team, the twelve lads at our pit were finally re-employed after months in the wilderness. This was a good day for us all, one little victory just to give NUM Branch officials the motivation to keep at it.

These small important victories gave an impression that things could turn out all right in the end, but they made no dent on the bigger picture. The relentless march of pit closures chipped away at any optimism. Over 80 pits were to close between the end of the strike and 1992. Everyone knew we would have to face up to a closure threat at our own pit eventually.

Yet it was another seven years before the final axe came and I for one had no option but to get on with the job. But which job? I was now an NUM Branch Official. Chasing machines up and down a coal face slowly became less of a priority. I stuck it out with my mates in the face team, but other pressures built up.

After about two years of trying to do union work and stay with the face team, I accepted the union job was more important. Working with the same team, but only two or three shifts a week, did no one any favours. It made deployment difficult. I went on the face market – a spare face worker when others did not turn up.

---

61 National Justice for Mineworkers.

I was uncomfortable in this role and I was exposed to deploying overmen getting their own back for previous bust-ups. As part of a regular face team, I was secure from provocation, but on my own it was harder. I was once deployed with a hacksaw to cut through the rails on a tub road in order to fit some points. Any reasonable person should know that this was a job for the surface workshops. Of course, the overman wasn't being reasonable – he was having a laugh at my expense. I spent all shift in the middle of nowhere sawing rails very slowly with the hacksaw. Not the best use of a face worker.

The same overman tried again and I was deployed to the downcast pit bottom to clean up. Under the Mines and Quarries Act, toilet areas are required underground. As far as I knew they were never used, but this dark recess near the coaling shaft was full of human shit and bog paper. I picked up a phone and refused to do the job. The overman had had his fun and I was redeployed elsewhere. The manager probably had no idea this type of petty behaviour was done in his name. Still, I was a grown man after all and being bullied like a school kid should not have bothered me. But it did. I had plenty experience of older, bigger lads giving me a hard time at school and that feeling cuts deep.

I could support NUM members much better on underground inspections and meetings with management than working on the coal face. It was not something I relished because it is easy to lose touch with the day-to-day issues, and an invisible gap opens up between you and your workmates.

Work now was divided into the usual graft of cutting coal and representing a workforce of some 800 people. Coming off shift usually meant a get together in the NUM office to catch up. I managed to avoid night shifts at this stage, which was a big bonus.

The NUM officials could now be found in a Portacabin across the pit yard from the baths and canteen. A number of pit top buildings had been knocked down. It was the manager's idea to save on rates to the Council. The office could get very busy, and between shifts it was a chance to exchange snippets of news and pit gossip.

Bonus pay, or lack of it, was a constant source of aggravation. The bonus system had changed several times since it was introduced in 1979 and management were always trying to claw back payment and still keep up production.

'No cash – no dash' was the usual response from the workforce, but that does not always pay dividends if the plan from upstairs is to run the pit down and close it. Discussions in pit meetings, discussions at area level came and went and gradually sapped the energy of all concerned.

Somehow everyone began to get the feeling it was all going nowhere. It was difficult to summon up a positive attitude when all around it seemed the vultures were gathering.

The day-to-day activity of the NUM at any pit is often mundane. It's a strange mix of health and safety issues and social work punctuated by the odd crisis. It can be a headache you really think you can do without.

The Branch Secretary opens a filing cabinet and pulls out some current compensation claims. He checks on the most recent correspondence and makes a note in a dog-eared book on his desk. Three of the men on file have had offers made and he needs them in the office to discuss whether to settle on the terms offered or push for more. Seems about the right kind of offer to him but some lads like to chance their arm and always think they are being robbed. It's a fair reaction for people struggling to make ends meet.

The filing cabinet is heaving with a couple of hundred claims of one sort or another. Each has to be carefully monitored and the lads kept up-to-date. The Branch Secretary's time is dominated by the administration of litigation from black thumbnails to missing limbs. 'Eyes, top whack' as they say. In addition to various accidents, industrial disease compensation claims from the DHSS filled yet more filing cabinets.

In my time at this colliery, I had not had to deal with fatalities, but a mate was killed at a nearby pit before the strike. The deceased was a fitter who, whilst crawling on the face side to a broken-down machine, was crushed when a section of the six-foot-high coal face toppled sideways onto him.

I had met him on the Miners' Day Release course at Sheffield University. Considered by some to be just another excuse to avoid work, the course was a great forum for sharing experiences and kicking around political ideas.

Another funeral – one of many as the years passed by.

Not long after I started work on the face, I had to help carry out a mate with, what turned out to be, a dislocated hip bone. The hip and pelvis had become separated. A lump of stone had flashed out and pinned him at the back of the last steel arch set in a main gate. Despite being pumped full of pethidine, the mate screamed all the way out of the pit on a very uncomfortable stretcher being manhandled down tight roadways and bumpy paddy rides.

Some years later as an NUM official I visited an accident site with an HMI (Her Majesty's Inspector of Mines.) An older development worker had had his leg ripped off by a block and tackle chain that got caught on an armoured conveyor. There wasn't much that could be concluded except perhaps don't try to lift heavy machinery over a moving conveyor. The bloke's leg had been carried out of the pit in a bag full of frozen chips and vegetables from the canteen. Clever thinking perhaps – but the plan did not work. He lost his leg and had to settle for financial compensation. Another very big file to flick through.

Another day, another list of tasks with no obvious reward. Can't complain, you may think – it's surely better than working for a living. Walking across the squeaky lino, the files are returned to the cabinet and everything seems in hand. The Branch Secretary will ring the Barnsley office later and make a few enquiries about stalled cases. Drinking lukewarm tea, the union men exchange knowing glances.

"I want you in the office next Monday," said the Branch Secretary just before knock off.

"You want me … What the hell for?" I replied, taken aback and grouchy as usual. It was not on my agenda and I did not appreciate the working week being re-organised by someone supposed to be a mate.

"There's a bit of a storm brewing over bonus payments and we need to see the manager before it gets out of hand," he added to explain the request.

"I am expecting some of the lads going on afters to come in here and give us a roasting – they have a strong case from where I'm standing. We need to meet the manager mid-morning and try and sort something out."

The Branch Secretary had all the figures to hand but winning an argument with management was becoming a rarity.

"Well, OK then," I conceded and began re-planning the following week in my head. Your life wasn't your own. Somehow you were there to help others and you had not noticed the shift from manual work to public service. Thinking back, chasing a coal face machine seemed so much more straight forward.

Nothing to be done but just get on with it.

As Branch Delegate it was my job to attend monthly NUM Area Council meetings in Barnsley and any conferences. This included the Annual Conference, which was usually held in a seaside town. Once again, you become easy prey to those who liked to moan about where their union subs were being spent. There was a half-joking assumption that the Branch Officials had some kind of expenses fund stashed in the office. Going on shift lads would call into the office to sort out some issue and ask:

"Where's tin? Where's t'cash? Been dipping' in tin again?"

"Come on, let's have the cash!"

"Scutch, there is no cash … drop it," I pleaded to no avail.

"No kidding, that's not what I heard," grinned Scutch. "Come on giz a shift in the office … I can mash the tea, anything yer like."

Humour and irony – piss-taking – it's the only safety valve between peace and war in a male work environment.

A downside of all the shifts I was not deployed on a face or development was that I earned much less productivity bonus. The hourly rate was guaranteed, but nothing else. So, the tin would have come in handy if it had actually existed. You can't have it both ways it seems. Incomes for coal miners were very varied depending on bonus and overtime. The popular view of the well-paid jobs in the pits was misleading. The basic wage, even for face workers, was nothing much to shout about. Picking out a payslip for 1991 I noted weekly earnings came to around £280 with about £40 incentive/bonus included. Take home pay: £210. In the privatised coal industry of the late 1990s, £1,500 per week was not uncommon.

My first weekly pay packet from the pit in 1977 was about £36 take home. I had been used to taking home over a hundred quid a week sub-contracting some years before. I then worked on the gas grid as a fitter's mate around South Manchester and Cheshire. I had no training to work on gas pipelines, but there were few questions asked when it came to sub-contracting and not much attention paid to health and safety. All that was needed was a paid-up trade union membership card and the TGWU obliged. The pit was a very different world where regulations were strictly adhered to.

When not deployed on the usual mining duties I was expected to carry out pit visits, inspections. Then of course there were the meetings … sometimes meetings about meetings. It was a different routine, but a routine nevertheless.

Being an NUM official had its little perks. On one occasion the Branch officials were allowed to organise a visit of friends and family to the pit and go underground on a working face. This was something few 'civilians' ever got the chance to do. As it turned out the face we toured was manned that shift by my former team.

On arriving at the tail gate, the party flopped on their knees and crawled via the wind hole[62] onto the face and along the chock track. The face was at a standstill due to a problem with outbye conveyors. A slow crawl now, but unusually quiet with no falling ground or clouds of dust. Through the chit chat came some musical accompaniment over the face Tannoy.

"Free, free, free, Nelson Mandela!" an impromptu choir in the main gate filled the air.

All the visitors except me were puzzled. I knew only too well they were taking the piss with this popular song of the time and most definitely not showing support for Nelson Mandela. My views on black freedom movements were not shared by some of the work mates.

To this day my partner, Caroline, well remembers the trip and, because the face was at a standstill due to a breakdown, she can't resist taking the piss about miners sitting on their arses most of the time, occasionally singing.

---

62 Short opening at tail end of a retreat face for ventilation and men and material access to the coal face.

○ ○ ○

Most visits were not for recreation – safety and productivity were the two main goals with two main provisions. The first was under the Mines and Quarries Acts. These were statutory inspections and the reports were sent to the Inspectorate of Mines (HMI). The second was part of the nationalisation structure, which built in consultative arrangements between management and trade unions to iron out production problems and foster co-operation. As a branch official I was involved in both.

At British Coal Area HQ I was given training in the safety inspector role. It was a short course designed to reinforce much of what I already knew. But amongst other things there was a fair bit about gas and miners' flame safety lamps. When the class was asked what anyone knew about gas, the bloke next to me chimed in:

"Yorkshire puddings – gas mark seven!"

"Very good young man," replied the instructor. "Now fucking button it or you are off the course!"

It was a little surprising that the instructor was so intolerant, but even more surprising that a miner knew anything about cooking Yorkshire puddings. Surely most miners were the worse for beer in the club on Sunday afternoons, not slaving over a hot stove.

It is a popular misconception that miners' lamps are for seeing in the dark. They are in fact for detecting mine gases and, in particular, methane. Colliers' lamps detect gas but cannot be re-lit. Only mine officials (deputies and overmen) carry the proper lamp for accurate mine gas detection. This is done by setting a small test flame in the lamp and placing it in an area to test for gas.

Different makes of lamp have slightly different gas cap shapes but the principle remains the same. It is possible, with practice, to spot the particular flame shapes for differing levels of methane from nil to twenty per cent. As a workmen's inspector I did not carry a safety lamp; I preferred to carry an electronic methane detector that could be read in an instant.

It is also a common mistake to think canaries had no place in a modern coal mine. Under provisions of safety legislation, every mine kept canaries, even if they were never used.

This safety job was known more commonly as a 123 inspector. The odd name relates to Section 123 of the Mines and Quarries Act. These Acts of Parliament codified decades of health and safety knowledge and procedures in mines and quarries.

The inquiry into the Wharncliffe Woodmoor Colliery disaster of 1936, in which my uncle was closely involved, will have played a role in drawing up the safety codes. As would all other disasters and major incidents. The Acts were a product of bitter experience, lessons from mistakes and cock-ups coupled with scientific method. The loss of life in UK coalmines was a national disgrace until slowly the law was brought in to enforce safer working practices. It's not that explosions could no longer ever happen – they did – but they were much less likely in the tighter safety regimes developed after nationalisation.

I took the safety part of the job seriously. Some years after I had left the pit, the first sight of the pencil-written observation notes of my uncle jolted the brain. The notes were so old and yet so very familiar. I saw in an instance what they were, but took a little time to believe my own eyes. Not significant to most people perhaps, but real history on scraps of dirty paper.

Safety inspections took place in every corner of the pit on the surface and underground. Thankfully it was usually an 8am ride down the shaft, allowing a bit more time in bed. My mates would have concluded, once again, I was dodging work.

I usually accompanied the deputies' union secretary, someone from the safety staff and someone from management. Occasionally an area NUM Inspector would tag along and on the odd occasion an inspector from the HMI. This would usually happen if there was a problem that the inspector had seen in reports and he wanted some input. A serious accident would bring the HMI down like a ton of bricks.

Notebooks and pencils are tools not usually associated with coalmining but there is a lot of note taking – observations, 'to do' lists, memos. A top pocket in the jacket or very often a waistcoat pocket, especially with deputies, was very useful. So many bits of information. Flicking back through an old notebook caked in grime, I pondered on my own scribblings from a visit:

S30's – 3.10. 89

1. Supply gate – Outbye – lights for points not working.
2. Fire-fighting equipment required.
3. Triangular bandages needed in First Aid Box – eyewash same.
4. 950-metre refuge hole not deep enough.
5. Stone dust required.
6. No guard on haulage return wheel.
7. Transport Rules Board required Inbye.
8. Panzer tail end needs a guard.
9. Loader Gate First Aid box – replenish.
10. Fire hoses need to be further Inbye.
11. Transport Rules for Loader Gate also required.
12. Outbye Loader Gate – fire buckets need re-filling with sand.

This mundane list seems to add up to very little. However, each little slip in standards had potential hazards waiting. The persistence of reporting and re-reporting, nagging and cajoling went some way to reducing potential disasters. The rules were there for a reason. Keeping problems 'in house' and getting them sorted at pit level was the approach usually taken.

If a serious accident did happen, then the inspector would turn up – not something management relished.

I made the mistake once of telling an NUM national officer, an old friend, in a pub one night, that I had found an automatic methane detector taped up in a tail gate on an inspection. These detectors are supposed to pick up higher than normal methane levels and cut out the electrical power to the underground district.

Having surmised an electrician had 'defeated' the instrument because it was stopping production and causing hassle, I was not minded to report it and get an NUM member into trouble. Was it reading accurately? I did not know – but the detectors were a bit temperamental. With the tape removed I carried on the visit, only to foolishly mention it at the pub one evening.

I arrived at the pit NUM office oblivious to the repercussions. Sitting like a school headmaster to the left of the Branch Secretary was the NUM Area Safety Inspector. A former NCB manager, he had all the strut of a Guards officer.

The man glowered behind a cloud of fag smoke. The Branch Secretary let slip an occasional smirk. Seemed I was in trouble and everyone was having a laugh at my expense.

"OK … let's be clear, and I mean clear," the inspector began. He meant, I'm in charge and you pillocks listen and listen good! I have better things to do and I'm sure you must. "

"I have unofficially received a report of the deliberate defeating of a safety monitoring device. 'Deliberate' is not a word I like to hear when lives may be at risk."

A short pause. Some staring out of the window.

"Now where do we go from here?"

"None of this has gone through channels – so let's keep it that way. I don't want to waste my time and effort following up chit chat in the alehouse for crying out loud!"

"If you have something to report, report it – get the picture?"

I shifted from one foot to the other and was just beginning to get narked but thought better of it.

"Fine, excellent, I think we are now on the same page. Let's move on – we are all in this together," concluded the inspector getting ready to leave.

"Where have I heard that before?" I mused.

The inspector lit another fag, walked ramrod-backed to the door and left.

"Oh, nice one!" the Branch Secretary uttered, finally discovering his voice and grinning from ear to ear.

The pit and area consultative processes had been established for decades and seemed to encapsulate a co-operative, non-confrontational ethos in the coal industry. 'All in this together' springs to mind once more. I was on the pit Consultative Committee before being elected as a branch official. It made perfect sense to meet up with management before the strike to discuss how to solve the pit's problems.

After the strike and late in the 1980s that feeling of being 'all in it together' faded even further. Management could not hide the fact they were under much more pressure and that pressure filtered down the chain of command. At some meetings it was out-and-out aggression from some clever dick managers. Some of them could not resist flaunting their superiority. At other meetings there was sullen resignation from both sides that whatever anybody did it would never be good enough.

Many pit managers had a genuine interest in the future of the industry – they were loyal 'coal people' and no friends of the Tories. But none ever made a stand; they had too much to lose. An older manager had a very comfortable superannuation to come as the pits closed. They knew that what was happening was wrong but their retirement pot was too important.

Each setback underground would result in rants from some quarter or another. Pit planning flipped to short-termism and mistakes could be seen a mile off. Yet our pit was still getting away with it and the grim reaper always seemed to turn elsewhere. Nevertheless, longer-term plans were notable by their absence. Plans for the next four faces seemed to stack up but what then? Neither outside contractors, nor the area drivage team, was being prepared for opening up new areas of coal.

Around two hundred collieries were operational at the start of the 1984 strike. By 1991 this had fallen to about sixty.

As meetings, pit visits, and inspections came and went it was easy to get sucked into the belief that, despite the occasional venom from management, it was all worthwhile and there could be a good outcome. Sitting in their temporary portacabin, the NUM Branch officials didn't fully realise that it was temporary for a reason. When you're keeping busy and giving off an air of purposeful activity, each day is a bonus. Taking a deep breath, you couldn't help but wonder what shit was coming our way.

There was a lot to think about and it was frustrating the workforce seemed to have so little control of our destiny. Meetings with management were often an exercise in blatant blackmail. Just to rub it in, the pit was in the Colliery Review Procedure every time production dropped off. But it backfired on the miners' morale. Some people were just looking for a way out.

"Do as you are told or the pit shuts!" was no idle threat when pit after pit is shutting across the country. Older miners left and transferees from nearby closing pits took their place. There was a constant churn of manpower and problems multiplied. Ingrained responsibilities were replaced by a 'who gives a fuck' mentality.

"The future of the pit is in your hands!" was the management mantra.

But that's just it – it's never been in in the hands of the workforce! British Coal and their bosses in government were making their plans but sharing nothing with the workforce. The plans involved them taking over and personally cashing in – the future and UK energy policy were far from their concerns.

This is what happens when you lose the biggest strike in a generation.

11

FACING UP TO CLOSURE

It was a road race like many others. A bit of anxiety in the hour before the start. Lots of fit-looking people and some not so fit-looking. We three Yorkshire miners started together but soon lost sight of each other.

"Just keep an eye on the kilometre markers and see how you feel at halfway," I muttered to myself.

Coming through twenty kilometres I'm thinking, "This is not so bad. Just keep it like this and you will be under three hours." I keep the pace but then have a blip for what seemed like an age. Legs heavy, I begin to doubt. One or two runners pass as I slow a little. A drink station results in a better frame of mind and most of the hard work is done.

The finish line at last! A bit of nausea as I put in a final effort and then slump forward with hands on sweaty knees staring at the tarmac for few seconds surrounded by other runners at varying levels of distress and euphoria.

"Well, I could have done better, but it's a good time in the circumstances."

A British Coal Area Director, Bob Siddall, had presented me with a small bronze-looking prize for the mantelpiece. As part of a three-man British Coal team, we had beaten our German equivalent, Ruhrkhole (RAG), in the Essen Marathon. It was a three-day jolly to the Ruhr with all the meat you could eat

– vegetarians beware the hospitality of German miners! In those days I ran marathons in under three hours usually, which was good enough on this occasion to help beat the German team. It came as a surprise to me when I was told I had qualified for the team in the Potteries Marathon in June earlier that year.

The trip had been organised by CISWO – the Coal Industry Social Welfare Organisation. The handshakes and pleasantries on the occasion of the presentation from the Area British Coal boss seemed to convey some measure of humanity and consideration for others. For a brief moment the troubles of the coal industry were not on the agenda.

That same Director wrote to me in glowing terms on 2 January 1992:

"I have recently heard about your notable performance in the
above marathon (Essen).

From the comments I have received I understand that you were an
excellent ambassador for British Coal in general and
South Yorkshire Group in particular.

On behalf of the Corporation I would like to offer my congratulations
and thanks for your efforts while taking part in this event."[63]

Despite the afterthought of a (very late) letter of congratulations, the damage had already been done weeks before. The same director had summoned the Thurcroft NUM Branch to Area HQ at Allerton Bywater, in November 1991. A press release from the Area Director outlining the prospects for all South Yorkshire collieries ominously singled out our pit and one other. That other pit was Hatfield. It survived this review, was privatised in 1994 and did not close for another twenty-four years.

Our pit was struggling with a new heavy-duty face that was taking too long to get into its stride. A second new face was yet to be kitted up. The shiny white chocks were stacked on the surface – Immediate Forward Support or

---

63 Letter from South Yorkshire Group Director, 2 January 1992.

IFS chocks – some new kit at last. But they were never used and sent to another pit in the South Yorkshire Group.

Anyone looking at the books for this period would have concluded the pit was a dead loss, yet a few months earlier the pit was on song. It was not difficult for the conspiracy theory to arise that this was deliberate planning to show the pit in a bad light and close it in the lead up to privatisation, which was to come at the end of 1994.

The Director spoke solemnly and in a measured fashion as he told the four NUM officials at the review meeting the pit should close in the first week of December, 1991. A different kind of 'presentation' and a nice Christmas gift for hundreds of miners and families.

The reasons given for closure by the Director were relayed via the colliery manager in a letter to everyone:

a   *The colliery has lost over £11 million in the year so far.*

b   *This loss is bound to increase, probably to over £15 million, by the end of March 1992.*

c   *We are encountering severe geological problems on our only face – K6's in the Swallow Wood Seam. The Director saw no real prospect of this geology improving in the near future. Any alternative plans would only increase the financial losses.*

d   *Over the past year we have seen growing evidence of geological difficulties in the Haigh Moor Seam – the effects of swilleys[64] on L04s are well known to you all. It is likely that no better results would be achieved from 5s or 30s which are also affected by the continuation of the swilleys.*

Clearly, the present weekly losses of £300,000 cannot continue.
Sadly, there is no alternative to prompt closure.

---

64 Where a coal seam dips steeply and then rises again making it difficult to follow with a machine. Often caused by streams and rivers in the ancient geology.

The letter makes no mention of L12s, a face that could be up and running in weeks and had no adverse geology. On paper there were plans to work at least eleven more faces taking production up to 1998. However, British coal was in a mad rush to get this pit shut before the run-in to privatisation

The television news cameras gathered around the NUM officials as we walked back to our cars. There was no comment – the news was not ours to blurt out but needed to be relayed to those back at the pit. The miners and their families had plenty of media snippets to feed off, but nothing official. We NUM officials kept our own counsel and had planned a meeting for the next day to pass on all relevant information.

But the pit manager scuppered the plan and was already holding his own meetings pre-shift in the canteen. The 'big sell' of redundancy payments was underway and the skids were under the union's attempts to resist British Coal plans. This was now a well-trodden path. Under the terms of the Colliery Review Procedure agreed at the end of the 1984–85 strike, British coal was required to give ninety days' notice of closure. But if the workforce could be persuaded to accept British Coal's offer, including early closure, then all the better for them – no notice was required.

Striking miners had endured twelve months of hardship to stop any miner voting to shut another miner's pit – now here they were on the brink of shutting their own pit and destroying jobs for ever.

The days that followed were hard to take as everyone had their own agenda. I tried to tough it out. "Fuck 'em all, the lot of 'em ..." I thought, but the back-biting and resentment from those wanting to get out wore me down. Still, a collective decision was needed and the only way was to hold a pit-head ballot on whether to accept the terms or fight. The date was set and preparations made even though some at the pit wanted it over and done with immediately.

The workforce at the pit was swelled with transferees from other local pits. They had no particular loyalty to one pit or any respect for NUM officials they did not know. Overnight, my popularity as a union official plummeted. I stood in many people's way of a £30,000 pay off and whatever you had to say was now shouted down.

The NUM Branch hit back with a brief but intensive campaign to try to counter the impending rush for the lifeboats.

The key argument was made in leaflets and a letter distributed to everyone. Some of the text follows:

Following the Re-convened Meeting, the NUM placed the pit in the Modified Colliery Review Procedure[65]. British Coal have no right to cease production on 6 December, 1991, or alter the fabric of the mine.

They have to give us one month to reply. They have to continue with mining operations. They can only shut the pit if we co-operate with British Coal's proposals – British Coal are in breach of a signed, agreed procedure.

There is nothing inevitable about the closure. There is every chance of fighting the closure with your support.

If British Coal want to shut the pit – let them try – we should have no part in it. There are many men who want to continue work at the pit – do not help British Coal destroy their livelihood.

Posters appeared in the village with rats deserting a sinking ship. I had sanctioned this tactic and got help from Sheffield mates, but it had a mixed response and, on reflection, may well have been unhelpful.

That Sunday evening the Welfare was packed. National and Area NUM leaders were invited to try and build some momentum to resist management plans. Yet the gathered crowd were mainly the converted and a significant number were not miners from the pit but people from around South Yorkshire showing their support. For example, my partner and two of the kids sat in the audience.

It was a good meeting and a great feeling. 'Stand tall; let's have a go; we've nothing to lose!' was the sentiment.

But the key decisions lay with each individual at the pit. The branch meeting on the following evening was subdued – no one wanted to admit defeat,

---

65 Modified Colliery Review Procedure: the 'deal' struck with NACODS towards end of the 1984–85 strike.

but many men had already made up their minds and were not likely to share their thoughts.

"Great speech," a chock fitter confided in me after the meeting, "But I reckon it's all over – every man for himself – there is no future here."

The Branch stuck to its guns and held a pit-head ballot. The result was: about 55% voted to let the pit shut and 45% were still ready to carry on the fight. Many who voted to stick with the pit had gone back to work before the end of the strike. Others who remained loyal in the strike, this time voted to get out. There was a sense that the industry was going nowhere and for some, the job wasn't worth having any more.

With the decision taken, British Coal lost no time in processing the workforce who wanted redundancy. Interviewed by human resources, hundreds left before Christmas. Old mates, solid union men who had struggled for a year on strike against the odds just threw in the towel. Others opted to pick up the £4000 transfer money and moved to nearby pits. No one had won a battle to save any of the pits so it was easy to ask yourself, 'why waste time and effort trying?'

Solidarity, collective action and comradeship were replaced by short-term self-interest. There was no surprise in this and no condemnation, just sorrow as all that seemed worthwhile in the job evaporated and was replaced by uncertainty. For those like me, who had invested so much emotional commitment, the hurt cut deep. Hopelessness and conflicting allegiances replaced previous aspirations and comradeship. The drip, drip, drip of nagging doubts made every decision tainted with dark thoughts. What if … What might have been … If only …

A tiny silver lining to the dark clouds came with a letter from the Scottish international footballer, Gordon Strachan, who played for Leeds at the time. He donated the fee from his column in the regional paper, the *Yorkshire Post*, to the local union branch and expressed his solidarity with the families facing Christmas and an uncertain future.

As low as I could remember, I prepared for the seasonal festivities. Fake smiles and rosy cheeks on the television added to the gloom and smouldering resentment. No parties at the Welfare this year. Still there was always plenty of booze to get lost in.

My partner and young son went to Egypt. Friends who he went to school with in Sheffield had died with their father when an apartment block collapsed in Cairo. Caroline and Tom were visiting the mother.

I went to Whitby for a few days with my youngest, Annie, and other friends. There was some relief as the cold North East wind whistled around your head on an empty beach, eyes watering from the cold air. At least the wind was real and you couldn't buy it in a supermarket. A steel blue sky, grey stratus, other wisps of lower cloud and just a hint of pink at 3.30 in the afternoon. It would be dark soon enough and the incoming tide suggested I should move. Noisy seagulls broke my contemplation. I have a fondness for birds so, what is it about seagulls I find so annoying?

My partner and young lad turned up from their trip away to complete the group of friends. Too much alcohol and too much food. Nevertheless, a break straight after Christmas by the sea or in the hills always fed the soul.

This welcome diversion soon faded as I returned to work. With no coal production, all there was to do was salvage machinery. I found myself deployed on any number of jobs that seemed pointless. Every shift and every hour dragged. Nothing left but to kill time until the final closure date at the beginning of April. Waiting for that last shift, waiting for that final plunge into the dark and return to the light.

One last bit of drama – the upcast pit bottom had unusually high gas readings. It was concluded that the methane must be migrating from a nearby closed colliery, Treeton, along an old roadway in the Barnsley seam. Despite the pit being only a few weeks from final closure, the problem needed sorting. Stoppings were required at a number of locations to remedy the situation. Tonnes of stone dust bags were sent underground and the stoppings painstakingly erected. The irony was not lost on us as we manhandled heavy bags of stone dust into place just to give the pit a few more futile weeks of life.

There were so many reasons I did not want the pit to shut and so many other reasons I wanted an end to it. There was far too much time to think in those last few weeks as the hours dragged by. Too many circular arguments with no resolution.

"Coal? Who the hell wants coal?" I interrogated myself, staring at the four walls around me.

"This is a chance to change your life – get out while you have your health."

"No – I won't let them get me down. Not now – not after all we have been through."

Sitting at the table picking at the food and trying to get my mind in some kind of order, I found no good answers.

"Just let it go ... move on." My mind switched from rage to misery.

"If I hear the word 'coal' again in the next thousand years it will be too soon ... I for one have had enough!"

I settled on that view and waited for events to unfold. It did not take long.

Other people without the same baggage of despair and anger were taking small steps down a different path. Somewhere in a local council office, minds were coming together. They were seeking a way to take on pit closures through an entirely different route. If British Coal didn't want the pit, then maybe someone else did.

Who better to run the pit but the miners themselves? Phone calls were made. Little ideas soon became big ideas. Perhaps too big.

12

THE FUTURE WE BUILD[66]

With final closure fast approaching, a flurry of unseen activity emerged into the light. Lots of talk and good wishes. Unsure? Suspicious? Who can you trust? Does it matter now? What's the alternative?

'Let's get on with it!' seemed to be the sensible thing.

Following discussions with Rotherham councillors and officers, it was agreed to convene a meeting in the Miners' Welfare Hall. The project was initiated by Rotherham Council people through our NUM branch, but quickly widened to include anyone interested. The other local mining unions NACODS, and COSA[67] joined in and miners from other pits that had closed also participated.

The Welfare Hall had seen many meetings but this was arguably the most important. Did the pit have one last chance of survival? The proposal on the table was simple: was there enough support for a mineworker buy-out of the pit? There was plenty of expert advice on hand from Rotherham Council, Sheffield Hallam University Business School, the Sheffield Co-op Development Group and solicitors with expertise in employee share ownership.

---

66 Part of the NUM motto.
67 Colliery Officials and Staff Area.

The idea of a buy-out had not come out of thin air. Rotherham Council and some of its officers were active in the Coalfield Communities Campaign (CCC). This was a national organisation of local authorities in coalfield areas. The main interest was in the economic development and wellbeing of coalfield communities facing closures and job losses. This was the task and political focus that predated 'Levelling Up' by several decades. The Council had supported other pits in the Rotherham area in the Modified Review Procedure, but this had proved a dead end.

In Midlothian, south of Edinburgh, CCC and the local councils had helped bring together miners to start a co-operative at Monktonhall Colliery. The project had faced many difficulties but was up and running by 1992. They offered advice to the co-op project in Yorkshire and the Scottish manager visited and spoke at a meeting. They were particularly keen to buy any redundant mining machinery.

To be candid, I had so many reservations about the buy-out from the start, but my commitment to the pit and its workforce meant I would try to make the best of it. I no longer had any clear notion of what I might do. The default position was to keep working down the pit for a few more years and see how things went. I had done the job for fifteen years and my imagination about any alternatives failed me.

Plan 'A' was to put my name down for transfer to a pit north of Rotherham. It was a pit that topped the bonus earnings league and my thinking was that another year or two of higher earnings might not go amiss. Human Resources said no – again not living up to their pretentious title as usual. I was told I could go to Manton, a pit in the same British Coal group but geographically in north Nottinghamshire. I confess I did not fancy Nottinghamshire one bit and the daily commute was only part of my concerns. I was not interested in a job at any price. So, with a transfer off the table I had to reconsider the next move. The buy-out looked the best bet and appealed to my 'leftie' instincts.

In April 1992 there was to be a General Election. If nothing else, it was important to keep the pit open just in case Labour got into government and perhaps initiate a major re-think on pit closures. Maybe, just maybe, they might have a good look at energy policy, energy security and clean coal technology. Even if precious little support was given during the strike by the Labour leadership, they had made efforts to stop mass pit closures. For the first time in many years there was a genuine chance of a Labour Government – or so it seemed. Although a Labour Party member, I was very much a part-timer and I freely admit it was a flag of convenience that opened a few more doors for an NUM Branch Official. But this was a General Election where I had a very personal stake.

Never previously an enthusiast for parliamentary politics, I put that aside and worked in the constituency and elsewhere for a Labour victory. It was more fun than I thought and I enjoyed touring the South Derbyshire constituency of Tory MP, Edwina Curry, blurting out Labour slogans. I failed to stick to the script. A favourite slogan I nicked from one of the NUM mates was – 'Vote Labour and get beer through the gas pipes.' Now *that* was a manifesto promise guaranteed to win votes! You need a laugh sometimes. But of course, the joke was lost on some of the overly serious Labour activists.

Things were looking up – surely the Tories couldn't get in yet again? John Major was hardly a star turn. Neil Kinnock, the Prime Minister 'elect', turned up in a helicopter, USA-style, at a mass rally at Sheffield Arena, thousands cheered and the dizzying spotlights added to the heady atmosphere. Who was on the stage? Shirley Bassey? Tom Jones? Led Zeppelin or perhaps Pink Floyd? No, just Neil and Glenys Kinnock. So much anticipation, so much showbiz. Lights – camera – action!

But the glitz did not work and nor did the hard work on the doorsteps. John Major and the Tories got re-elected. How the hell did we blow that? Who on earth still votes Tory after all the shit of recent years? The litany of Labour failures was to return after the Blair years. Voters in former mining areas slowly but surely deserted Labour. Many years later, the 2019 collapse of the Labour vote should not have been a surprise.

For Kinnock, and later 'reformers' in the Labour Party such as Tony Blair, the miners' strike was to blame for the continued lack of electoral success. The view was that the strike had split the left and, even by 1992, the damage had yet to be repaired. This was the wrong premise and wrong conclusion as far as many were concerned. Blair was never on the left and the Labour Party followed him up a blind alley. Blair is considered by many pundits to be

Thatcher's greatest achievement. Not a medal most people would want hanging around their neck.

The General Election and the national political arena bore no fruit. It was case of 'do it yourself or nothing gets done.' For the pit buy-out team it was back to Plan A: buy the pit and run it as a co-op.

When the plan gathered pace, I put my doubts aside and was drawn closer to it, working hard to make a success of it. I had to look over my shoulder all the time at fellow NUM officials, especially at national level. Arthur Scargill was staunchly against any form of ownership other than 1947-style nationalisation. He seemed to be overly influenced by Soviet-style command and control.

At first, the Yorkshire Area gave full support. Recorded in the minutes of the NUM Yorkshire Area Ordinary Council Meeting of 24 February 1992, is the following agreed resolution:

This Yorkshire Area Council calls upon the NEC to give full support to the continued campaign to keep Thurcroft open, in line with the proposals put forward by Rotherham Borough Council and the local NUM Branch.

At the NUM Annual Conference in the summer of 1992 in Scarborough, I had no option but to challenge the orthodoxy of national policy. My contribution to the conference was to explain the motivation behind the buy-out and, with another Tory Government, why and how we had tried to save the pit. Yet again there was plenty of sympathy and understanding from the delegates, but no one wanted to step out of line.

The speech was fairly and accurately reported in the *Yorkshire Miner* newspaper of August 1992. At national level there was no such sympathy. Arthur Scargill's address to the 1992 Conference included the following comments:

Participation in management buy-outs won't protect our members, pits, jobs or communities. It seldom, if ever, has. Britain's miners have attempted buy-outs or cooperative ventures before – with disastrous results.

> In 1875 following the establishment of the West Yorkshire Cooperative Coalmining and Building Society in 1873, West Yorkshire miners together with North Staffordshire miners purchased Hayswood Colliery. The venture collapsed in 1876 and "all those who bought shares lost their money".
>
> In 1875 the South Yorkshire and North Derbyshire Miners' Associations purchased Shirland Colliery – backed by many supporters (almost the forerunners of today's Coalfield Communities Campaign). In 1876, the venture collapsed and the only return the Union obtained for its expenditure of £31,500 was £250!
>
> The cooperatives failed to recognise that they were operating in a 'hostile, capitalist environment' where both suppliers of goods and purchasers of coal had vested interests in seeing the ventures fail. It was partly these experiences that led to the M.F.G.B. recognising that the real answer to privatisation was public ownership and in 1947 the objective and the dream became a reality. Our forebears fought too hard for us to sacrifice nationalisation without a fight.[68]

In the NUM national newspaper, a reference made to the 'nightmare' of closure was the only focus, with nothing reported on the facts of the situation and the efforts by loyal NUM members to take the pit over. The reported interest of the UDM in possible buy-outs only served to further taint the project in the eyes of some NUM officials. The Ridley Report on de-nationalisation from back in 1977 also suggested pits may be run by buy-outs or co-operatives. This was not the kind of encouragement we wanted either.

For the buy-out miners, the point was to keep 'holes in the ground' open and have a job. Without a coal industry there was no union, whoever owned it. Surely miners having a share in their own pit and running it themselves was better than what had happened since 1947. Nationalisation saved the coal industry after the Second World War. But Margaret Thatcher ended up running the industry. That wasn't the dream of past leaders of the NUM or the Labour Party. This important point was given some further thought many

---

68 NUM Annual Conference 1992, Presidential Address.

years later when the assault on the miners and the people of coalfield communities was characterised as:

'Illegitimate use of state power, facilitated by state ownership.'[69]

Keeping the pit open was better than letting it close but the NUM's official position left no room to try different options. Co-ops had been tried in the 19th century and failed, but that need not be the end of it.

Scargill himself, as Yorkshire President, had proposed the NUM should invest its own money in Barrow pit and coke works near Barnsley when it was closing in the 1970s.

The Times reported on 1 November, 1975:

'Left wing Yorkshire miners' leaders are considering moving into private enterprise to rescue a loss-making coking plant near Barnsley.'

The article goes on:

Mr Arthur Scargill said last night – "we are not simply recommending the spending of money in order to pour it down the drain. We believe this plant can be made a commercial proposition that will put money into the union funds."

The notion of using the coking plant as an income source for the NUM is a curiosity in itself. But Scargill went further; a little later, he even suggested using Miners' Pension Funds to invest in the pits.

Not having support for the buy-out from my own national union officials saddened me but I understood the need for a united front to save what was left of the industry. I was disciplined enough to keep my concerns a matter for NUM debate and not to feed the right-wing press looking to split the labour movement and peddle the private free market. But that did not stop those willing to try and do whatever we could to keep the pit open.

Over two hundred and fifty ex-miners signed up and pledged £4000 from

---

69 Huw Beynon and Ray Hudson, *In the Shadow of the Mine*. 2021.

their redundancy money to launch the buy-out. A company was formed and I reluctantly became a director. My reluctance, as usual, was due to my personal pessimism. It was a trait I wished I could rid myself of as it was unhelpful and often rubbed off on other people.

But everything seemed possible if you just had some ambition, I thought, trying to gee myself up. After all, my forebears had been mine managers; I was just following in the family tradition. We in the buy-out team set about planning what to do with the manpower that had signed up whilst others went chasing finance.

A major problem for the pit was the lack of a working face, kitted up and ready to produce. It was like starting from scratch. In contrast, all the pits taken over at the time of privatisation at the end of 1994 were ready for coal production. That was the government and British Coal's plan: use public money to invest in the mines and then sell them to a private company to reap the rewards of the 'hibernated' investment. All the better if you and your British Coal management mates are the private company that takes over.

Getting the pit back into production would take serious money, but the market for coal was not the problem. The seams worked were mostly used for coking coal. This was a higher revenue product and the steel industry was happy to buy more locally than from Canada or Australia. The irony was the pit closure plans of the government and British Coal did not consider this market important. For years the NCB, then British Coal, focused on the power station market at the expense of other markets. British Coal was perhaps the best in the world at mining coal, but they weren't very good at selling it. It was a nationalised industry created to provide cheap energy for private firms and the nation as a whole.

The miners in the buy-out team were not impressed with the mining plan submitted because of its reliance on American-style short wall or 'intermediate' mining. Yes, it looked good for a quick fix – it was easier and less costly to kit up such operations – but it was not what these miners were used to. It was a deep mine with many more geological pressures than most US coal mines.

It also cost a lot just to keep the basic infrastructure and underground roadways safe and workable. It was this last issue that proved to be insurmountable without British Coal co-operation. The clock was ticking, headaches and problems were building up and the new company was not yet in a position to take over the mine.

The buy-out team worked hard to put together a credible package covering the detail of the mining plans, marketing and the legal structure and financing for employee ownership. Those miners who bought shares were kept in close touch with developments. It was all new to the participants, time consuming and daunting but the project had its own momentum and hours of unpaid work went into planning a future for the pit.

Other, private buyers were invited to the pit, but private mining companies in the UK were small with little available investment to scale-up to a British Coal mine. Investment possibilities in the co-op remained alive but British Coal lost patience. They demanded eye-watering sums to keep the pit open on care and maintenance. Six months later British Coal kept ten pits on care and maintenance for eight months with no questions asked to help smooth the Government route to privatisation.

It was simple arithmetic – the co-op could not afford to waste its meagre assets without any immediate prospects of acquiring the mine and getting into production. British Coal was intransigent and spiteful. Their senior managers had their own ideas about privatisation and this particular pit was not included in the plans.

The worker directors of the new company put it to a general meeting that it was not possible to meet British Coal demands and a decision was taken to pull out of the buy-out process.

The decision was taken reluctantly but the directors were not businessmen with deep pockets and Rotherham Council had no slush fund to keep the project afloat. There were no recriminations, just an acceptance that we had at least had a go and made some kind of effort to get a grip on our own destiny for a change. The miners hoping for a job saw it as yet another kick in the teeth from British Coal. But later events proved it was not impossible and it could have been a credible option.

British Coal was quick to shift the blame. A press release from British Coal HQ at Eastwood Hall had this to say:

British Coal has acted responsibly and professionally and rejects any suggestion there had been a breach of faith ...

In view of the Company's refusal to meet the care and maintenance costs, British Coal has no alternative but resume the shaft sealing operations ...

It would be improper to expect British Coal and its ongoing mining units in South Yorkshire to sustain the care and maintenance costs of a colliery in which it had no further operational interest.

The same press release alleges the NUM representative for the pit had accepted:

... the buy-out could not succeed after the NUM voted to oppose all forms of privatisation – including workers' buy-outs ...[70]

That press release manages to stoke resentment from miners at operational pits, put the blame on the NUM and the naivety and lack of professionalism of the co-op company in a few short sentences. Of course, no indication of British Coal's motivation and vindictiveness can be found.

The trouble for me was that I was never really sure one way or the other. I wanted it all to be so different. I lost sleep worrying about what more could have been done. The new company had raised hopes and expectations just to see them trashed.

The failed project was seen by both British Coal and the leadership of the NUM as evidence that this kind of approach did not work and was fanciful folly. Monktonhall, in Scotland, struggled on for a couple of years but, after an underground flood, succumbed in 1997 to the financial pressures of trying to run a big deep mine.

Alternative ownership models were to come and go before the coal industry's final demise. Nothing that the NUM officially did was able to influence the outcomes. It was left to others to salvage what they could of the industry. The NUM clung to its well-established policies but that did not provide any answers.

---

70 British Coal, Public Relations Press Release, July 28 1992.

During the closures announced by Michael Heseltine after October 1992 a very similar project in South Wales at Tower Colliery was set up. This time it did work. Tower did not get stung for care and maintenance costs and the pit went into production immediately. The NUM gave it its blessing and ten years of further coal mining, wages and wealth creation was available to at least one Welsh valley as a result.

As Wales Online reported in 2018:

Saved from closure by workers with a deep-rooted faith in what they were doing, Tower became the symbol for the miners' resistance in the 1990s. And in 2008, with coal reserves finally exhausted after 140 years of production, it was the workers themselves who decided it was time to leave.

Tyrone O'Sullivan, the former NUM Branch Secretary and Chair of the buy-out, told the Guardian Newspaper:

We were the only pit in Britain who worked the last ounce of mining we could – who wouldn't be proud of that?

"I am so proud to look back on it as we as a group of miners had done everything that other people thought couldn't be done.

It could be done and the naysayers were wrong. So wrong.

Hatfield Colliery near Doncaster was saved from closure by a management buy-out, as was Betws in South West Wales. The ownership of Hatfield went through a number of phases, but it was one of the last pits in the UK to close in 2015, having been discarded by British Coal. It had found itself over twenty years of extra life – something many pits could also have done, given the chance.

The short-lived buy-out at Thurcroft hardly registered in the history books despite its potential significance. Thankfully a film crew took an interest and turned up to record events as they progressed. The film director was a London leftie and had particular interest in new ways to challenge the over-bearing march of free market capitalism. Needless to say, the hour-long film got a late-night slot on Channel 4 and attracted perhaps only niche viewers[71].

It was a thought-provoking film and did record the efforts of the co-op for posterity, but few people ever saw it and the general public were none the wiser. Shots of the pit tip, spirals of dust in the wind and destruction of the surface buildings appeared like some dystopian sci-fi movie. Orson Welles as *The Third Man* also made an appearance at various points in the narrative, as did snakes and some very mysterious Buddhist monks involved in sand painting. All very meaningful no doubt – but we had no pit to show for it.

It was not the end of co-operative ventures for the ex-miners of the pit. A design team at Sheffield Hallam University wanted to help out during the Heseltine closure period in 1993 and suggested ex-miners could manufacture and sell gas fires. Calor gas fires were notoriously ugly and poorly designed, but the Hallam team had some swish alternatives for the modern market. Rotherham Council once more pulled together a project to employ ex-miners on the site of the recently closed pit. The plan was to make and sell upmarket Calor gas fires to people with big houses in the rural parts of the UK. *Country Life* adverts were mocked up.

The design part was sound, but once again, transforming ex-miners into entrepreneurs proved a step too far. Training was provided and a number of ex-miners got involved. But when it came to financing, the project hit the same brick wall as the pit did. The money required to get this particular business up and running was considerable and was beyond the level of risk any of the ex-miners were prepared to take. The funding gap remained un-bridgeable and for the second time these ex-miners were to discover that there are no worthwhile financial instruments or provisions in the UK to support collective ownership of businesses. It is frustrating to this day that the trade union and Labour Movement is is still so myopic about such possibilities.

Apart from trips to the National Coalmining Museum with the kids and grandkids,

---

71 *Between Times*, Marc Karlin, A Lusia Films Production for Channel 4, 1993.

I never went down a coal mine again. My last view of my own pit was during the buy-out phase when I took some prospective buyers on to the new face, which was waiting in vain to be kitted up. The face had stood well despite the delays since development. There was no doubt this coal face would have been successful. The pit was quiet and the air fresher than usual with no mining taking place – like a Sunday morning, in fact. Nothing seemed to be out of place because very little of the outbye equipment had been taken out.

A pit holding its breath until the shafts were capped, then filled and it breathed no more. Two concrete pads with a methane vent on top of the upcast shaft are all that remains. Thousands of metres of underground roadways and crushed coal faces lie unseen, but for some not forgotten. With time, it too will also be forgotten and no doubt present a mystery to future generations who will have not the slightest concept of what a coal mine was.

It was British Coal's policy to erase the physical presence of closed coal mines as quickly as possible. The wrecking balls arrived soon after the shafts were capped and the scrappers went to work removing any obvious traces on the mine surface.

Pit demolition, 1992. Acrylic on canvas.

© David J Parry.

13

PRIVATISATION, THE LONG GOODBYE AND COALFIELD COMMUNITIES

An attempt was made to hang on to my sworn oath to never have anything to do with coal again when the pit shut. I tried to remind myself of that every time the word coal was uttered. But I was caught in some kind of dream doomed to repeat itself. Falling, falling … you wake up in a sweat but nothing has changed. A shake of the head, a deep sigh, some quiet cursing – doesn't do the trick. A lifetime invisibly chained to coal communities.

Despite the oaths, I was up to my neck in coal industry issues and coalfield communities for another twenty-five years at work before retirement at 66.

The first thing on the agenda after the thwarted buy-out was travelling to Pakistan on a trek to K2 base camp. I was captured by the romance of climbing it but would never be good enough, or daft enough. I had enjoyed climbing, hill walking and mountaineering for many years and had visited the Alps and other mountain ranges since the end of the strike. A bunch of mates learnt the rudiments of mountaineering and flogged up and down 4000-metre peaks by the easier routes. Now I had the time and money to go further afield.

The K2 base camp trip was a success in every way except we never got to K2. The crossing of a high pass was abandoned by the organisers because of lack of snow. We re-jigged the trip and went up the Biafo Glacier to Snow Lake. Other trips to the Himalayas in India and Nepal as well the Andes, Tien Shan and Atlas ranges, were more successful. As far away from coal as possible, but mountaineering and mining have some similarities when it comes to adrenalin and occasionally big lumps falling on you. Getting out of bed at unearthly hours was also a common feature.

For a few months I was rudderless and believed I needed to further my education. I considered going back to college but did not really like the idea. I enrolled on a TUC computer course, but backed out of yet more A levels. Then, in this process of falling, I landed on my feet. A university researcher I had met during the buy-out attempt was looking for someone to help follow up research into coalfield communities. It was very topical at the time of the Heseltine closures and national uproar about coalfield communities. Somehow, I became that someone.

Four years and an MPhil degree later, another job came my way with the Coalfield Communities Campaign (CCC). I worked for over twenty years for this coalfield-based local authority association. I was losing the attachments to the pit and its village, but I was unable to shake my attachments to coal even when the industry passed into history.

For some years the coal industry was still making headline news. When Michael Heseltine announced 31 pit closures in the autumn of 1992, a national outcry stopped him in his tracks – for a few months at least.

Ten of the pits were earmarked for immediate closure. At Houghton Main, where my brother ended up working, the women stepped up. The re-ignited Sheffield Women Against Pit Closures group set up camp with women from the Dearne Valley and the local NUM branch. At the same time pit camps were set up at six other pits: Markham Main and Grimethorpe in South Yorkshire; Vane Tempest in Durham; Parkside in Lancashire; Trentham/Hem Heath in Staffordshire, and Rufford in Nottinghamshire.

Pit camps, or around-the-clock, seven days a week protest, was new in an industrial context. However, camps such as at Greenham Common and outside the nuclear submarine base at Faslane were familiar to the women's movement and also adopted by the environmental movement. *Shit, I would later reflect – this is what was needed at Orgreave!*

It was a form of protest with imagination and inventiveness that sidestepped the official union hierarchy. The experience of the women in the 1984–85 strike came to the fore. The women were much better at mobilising support and were not tied to the traditional view of what a trade union could or could not do.

A book produced by the women activists much later in 2018 celebrated the campaign. The General Secretary of the TUC, Frances O'Grady, had this to say:

Women Against Pit Closures was at the heart of the 1984–85 miners' strike and subsequent campaigns. When another Conservative government announced plans to close more pits in the autumn of 1992, once again women galvanised popular opposition. And they did so with dignity, determination and imagination.[72]

My son Tom, ten years old at the time of the protests, commented in the same book:

At the pit camp and demonstrations, I always felt part of something important. To a child it felt like something huge, so it was hard to understand how we couldn't win ...[73]

As a five-year-old, my youngest daughter Annie played her part:

I have an early memory of arguing with my brother about who would carry the placard with the name of our dad's pit at this march ... It's such a significant

---

72 Foreword by Frances O'Grady: *You Can't Kill the Spirit, the untold story of the women who set up camp to stop pit closures.* 2018.
73 *You Can't Kill the Spirit. The untold story of the women who set up camp to stop pit closures.* 2018.

part of our family history that I feel like I share so many memories with everyone involved, and I have a real sense of pride in being part of it.[74]

Week in, week out the women and children stood the course undaunted by the task, taking pains to include everyone in a host of different events to keep the momentum up. They were tireless, persistent, dogged, relentless, upbeat, fun-loving, positive, all embracing – a mirror on the human spirit. How else could a hot air balloon demonstration have been organised? Certainly not by the officials at the NUM HQ in Barnsley.

In the 1992–93 fight against pit closures, the women and kids were the front runners and the men at the pits, facing an uncertain future, only too thankful for the help and positive publicity. A different pit and a different village, but Caroline and her mates lived up to the pit camp banner – *You Can't Kill the Spirit.*

Following close on the heels of the Heseltine closure episode of late 1992 until the summer of 1993, the industry was trimmed down for privatisation. Government White Papers and Select Committee Inquiries provided me with work at the Coalfield Communities Campaign, but did little other than postpone the inevitable. The 'ultimate privatisation' was now in the Tories' grasp.

On 1 January 1995 the coal industry passed into private hands, exactly 48 years since vesting day of nationalisation in 1947. Finally, the Tory Government policies had achieved the prize of privatising coal and slain the dragon of trade union militancy.

Back in 1947 the signs on each colliery read: *'Managed by the National Coal Board on Behalf of the People.'* It was a great step forward from the days of the callous mine owners. However, it had its drawbacks when the effective manager was a vindictive Tory Prime Minister. For all the positives, especially health and safety, it was far from a triumph of workers' control, and the people at large had little say in it either. In fact, it was managed to provide cheap energy to private industries so they could make a profit and sustain post-war growth.

---

74 op. cit.

A group of senior British Coal managers, including the Director who shut Thurcroft pit, schemed to take over the remaining profitable pits and opencast sites. They were to be bitterly disappointed when RJB Mining took the lion's share and they, after all their meticulous scheming, got nothing.

Richard Budge, the larger-than-life figure who owned RJB Mining, had a swagger and approach unfamiliar to the coal industry. He courted publicity, but fiercely defended the industry unlike the shackled government 'yes men' of British Coal. His portfolio of pits on lease and licence were well equipped and there was plenty of easy coal to mine. Thanks to Heseltine, the industry had contracts with the power generators until 1998. It was money for old rope for a few years at least.

Other buyers rescued some of British Coal's discarded pits and for a year or so the industry expanded for the first time in decades. Re-opening pits was unheard of. However, the new super pit at Asfordby in the Midlands encountered major geological problems and closed in 1997.

Coal Investments, a new company formed by a former British Coal marketing director, ran four previous British Coal mines but then went into receivership in 1996. There were also management buy-outs at two other pits.

In Scotland, Monktonhall soldiered on until 1997 under a private owner. Mining Scotland ran the big Longannet complex with the NUM and Scottish TUC on the Board. It closed after a flood in 2001. Opencast mining was the mainstay of the industry in Scotland for many years afterwards

In 1998, as the coal contracts were about to end with the electricity supply industry, I was once more involved trying to keep the industry alive. Through the All-Party Parliamentary Coalfield Communities Group of MPs, concerted campaigning and lobbying resulted in the Labour Government providing aid to the industry. A former NUM officer, MP and friend, chaired the Group and I provided the administrative back up. Apart from long days in London, I felt happy in this role and, for a change, confident in my abilities. My background in coal provided me with the credibility I needed in places where it was easy to feel out of your depth.

The aid package was implemented under European Union regulations on State Aid, something the Tories had refused to do in their long reign through the eighties and nineties. An Operating Aid package followed by an Investment

Aid package extended the life of a number of the mines. The financial instruments had different names, but it was an old-fashioned subsidy – something the coal industries in Germany and Spain had relied on for decades. It wasn't the EU that was killing off the UK coal industry; it was successive governments in Westminster.

However, the UK pits could not compete with opencast and imported coal. Although the use of coal in power stations was maintained at high levels, less and less was from UK deep mines. The UK was losing out environmentally and economically. Government energy policy was tied to market principles and the power suppliers had all their own way raking in huge profits.

The so-called 'dash for gas' often dominated the debate in the 1990s. The rapid expansion of new gas-fired power stations was restricting the coal market. In truth there was plenty of scope for UK coal, because gas remained expensive and increasingly in short supply. Ironically, Europe's dependence on gas was to have serious repercussions after Russia invaded Ukraine in 2022.

My first big job working for coalfield local authorities was to present evidence to oppose the building of a gas-fired power station in North Lanarkshire. A predecessor had done most of the leg-work to gather evidence. Thrown into the deep end, I was sent to the Public Inquiry in Cumbernauld.

It was a blessing to be a rookie on this occasion going toe-to-toe with top barristers for PowerGen, the big electricity supply company, though I had plenty of help from Scottish Coal and Scottish Power, a rival electricity supply company. The commercial interests of Scottish Power and the coal industry briefly coincided.

There were gasps and frowns when, giving evidence, I referred to the PowerGen QC as 'my learned friend'. A real howler apparently – only QCs can refer to each other as 'Learned Friends'. Scumbags from Barnsley just don't know the etiquette. The power station was never built. Nor was another planned in Fife. I was asked to help the local authority on that occasion as well. I spent many hours in Fife building a case to restrict the expansion of gas-fired power-generation. Coalfield local authorities were all still fighting a rear-guard action to keep the coal industry alive.

RJB Mining became UK Coal and Richard Budge was side-lined. It too became accountant driven, and focused on opencast and the property market.

When the decision to shut the Selby Complex was made in 2004 everybody could see it was now just a matter of time until the industry was completely closed down.

The Selby coalfield was opened as part of the 1970s 'Plan for Coal.' Altogether the five-pit complex only lasted 21 years. The pits were connected by underground roadways to a huge drift bringing coal to the surface. Most of the easiest coal was taken first. Why would a private company bother about what might happen 10 or 20 years into the future? No attempt was made to exhaust the available coal or work other seams. The cost of the big drift and coal preparation facilities was borne by five pits. When it was down to four, three and then two, the sums did not add up.

After talking to an NUM National Official, working for Coalfield Communities Campaign (CCC), I helped the union put together a case to keep the complex open. The NUM wanted to be taken seriously so opted for expensive consultants. In truth we at the CCC could have done the job for nothing, but we were seen as biased. The local Labour MP was supportive but opted to fight for the best redundancy and training package rather than try to stop the closures. He clashed with me in a local television interview. Few words have been exchanged since. Amusingly, he branded me 'an un-reconstructed Scargillite', which I took as a back-handed compliment, even if it was well wide of the mark.

Another milestone in the long-drawn-out closure process, was the demise of the big colliery Daw Mill near Coventry. This pit could turn out three million tonnes from one face, but the huge kit used meant face-to-face transfer of equipment was time consuming and costly. It was an underground fire that led to the mine being abandoned.

Chatting to a national official in the pit managers union (BACM) I was told the fire was entirely predictable. Daw Mill had very thick seams and some coal had to be left to collapse into the gob. When a face was finished, it needed to be salvaged and then closed off to restrict the air. Because of time constraints, this did not happen and new kit was installed on a new face. With air (oxygen) still circulating to the now redundant face, spontaneous combustion occurred. Thankfully everyone got out before the whole pit was engulfed. The pit was abandoned, along with equipment worth around £100 million.

The fire raged for months until it finally ran out of oxygen.

The CCC work drew me ever closer to all the problems of a dying industry. The job was to continue to put the case for coal and defend jobs. Investment in new, cleaner power stations, carbon capture and storage, a balanced energy policy, energy security, were all thrown into the mix. Successive governments failed to come up with any energy policy, leaving it to the private sector in the main.

As secretary to the MPs Group, I liaised between coalfield Members of Parliament, ministers, civil servants, trade unions and local authorities in coalfield areas. This involved setting up meetings, writing reports, and any number of administrative jobs. I mainly sat in the background nudging and cajoling where necessary and, where possible, trying to knit together an industry much more tuned to conflict and tub-thumping.

Following the minor success of attracting state aid the MPs' group was involved in promoting 'A Manifesto for Coal'. The initiative was, in name at least, supported by all the players, of course with the major omission of the government. It was no easy job to get such a disparate group together. Not much came of it, but at the time it had all the trappings of an industry-wide alliance presenting a reasoned case.

Next to Westminster Hall in The Grand Committee Room, coal industry people gathered for a meeting called by the Coal MPs group. Grand surroundings and grand ambitions. Unknown to the posse of NUM representatives, in attendance there was a small group of miners from Daw Mill (Warwickshire), a colliery with mainly UDM members. CCC had received a phone call from Daw Mill miners asking if they could attend. I wasn't going to stop them. But then I wasn't going to make a song and dance about it either. I knew the potential repercussions, but the industry was in its death throes and maintaining divisions and rancour would not help.

With no comment made, NUM representatives and UDM representatives sat in the same meeting. Some of the NUM perhaps did not realise who else was there. I was nervous, but thankfully some joint sense of purpose to defend employment in the coal industry brought about a fleeting moment of unity. It is what happened, but it was not something I wanted to dwell on – it wasn't the time to rake up enmity and bitterness from the strike.

At each step of the way to the final closure of the deep mines there I was with many others, putting in the effort, contesting every closure, rehearsing and reliving regrets for what might have been. But it became clear I was out of step with reality, sucked into a world where everything was behind me and nothing lay in the future.

Ironically there was a spurt of interest in new coal mines before the last deep mine shut in 2015. Plans were revealed to open a pit on the Cumbria coast. An Australian firm was looking to access coking coal. The government and county council were in favour and the plans were controversially still in place in 2023 when the government appeared to give them the nod of approval. The planned mine, those in favour and opponents, air their views regularly in the media. However, with a planet-ending crisis looming, the sectional interests and simplistic profit-and-loss economics no longer seem remotely important. Energy supply issues change. Climate change and the political climate are interwoven. Man-made calamities, including wars, add to the uncertainty.

In 2014 a project to open a new coal mine at Crofton near Wakefield in West Yorkshire emerged. The New Crofton Co-op Colliery put miner-owned pits back on the agenda. Perhaps the irony was lost on everybody but me. The company did all the preparation and put on a brave face despite the huge difficulties. Working for the CCC, I was interviewed by the BBC on the plans and took the opportunity to wish them well. It was like going back over a decade. However, the coal market position went from bad to worse and the project stalled. The environmental arguments against coal outweighed any possible social or economic benefit.

Slowly edging to a quiet end with the closures of Thoresby and Kellingley in 2015, few people in the UK even knew a coal industry still existed.

The people who did know and cared about coal's part in supplying energy were activists in the green lobby. 'Coal not Dole' was the slogan of the 1980s activists. Yet the sentiments shifted 180 degrees to seal the fate of the UK coal industry. Mining and using coal became anathema to left-of-centre progressives and green campaigners. There were few miners to take pity on. Criticism of the coal industry and opposition to the use of fossil fuels became the mainstream view. Fighting pit closures was all well and good back in the day, but it was now out of step with history.

I became convinced many years ago that capitalism and energy policy was oxymoronic. I also accepted many of the arguments of the green lobby, but a lifetime engrossed in coal and coal communities made it hard. Taking the piss came naturally to me and I would sometimes adopt a pseudo-scientific air and explain to the green lobby that coal was a renewable source of energy – you just had to wait a few million years.

For a time it seemed that the Labour and trade union movement were no longer seen by many people as relevant – a washed-up anachronism. All well and good for nostalgia and epic tales of yesteryear, but not much use in the modern world. Class, it seems was no longer a useful concept with which to understand society. For many, Marx was a 19th century has-been. The moral compass was still much the same for many of us, but it became harder to navigate. A so-called 'culture war' replaced the class war that had been so evident. So much more information, so much more media and social media dominance – it became very easy to just get lost. Who were the good guys? Who were the bad guys? Social, political consciousness is replaced by rankings on social media. Social media trolling became the pastime of saddos from the right and left. The splintering of ideological positions, taken for granted a few decades ago, gathered pace. Unseen hands, some government, some billionaires, were manipulating millions of people.

Without an energy policy that provided coal with a role, even the once most profitable pits were forced to close. Then in 2015 the Tory government announced that coal would no longer be used to generate electricity in the UK from 2025.

In 2015, for a few hours a day, it was the first time since the 1880s there was no coal being used to supply electricity – this became the norm. Only two years previously, coal was contributing thirty per cent of the power to the UK grid. Coal's use quickly faded away. With no incentive to re-fit, or even spend money on maintenance, coal-fired power stations began to close in quick succession. In the UK at least, the era of coal, first mined in the Middle Ages, was rapidly coming to a close.

Back in the 1970s the NCB was at the forefront of the development of what was loosely called 'clean coal technology'. 'Cleaner' coal technology might have been a better term. This underlying theme – how to use coal as cleanly and efficiently as possible – had animated some in the NUM years before the strike, during the strike and decades afterwards. Cleaning up all forms of energy and industrial production remained a figment of the imagination of boffins working on carbon capture.

Leaving aside the political vendetta of the Tories, it was the only way to provide any future for the industry and its communities. It wasn't just *one* possibility – it was the *only* possibility. Who wasn't getting this? Just about everyone it seemed as Tory and Labour governments took turns to ignore the obvious.

The outcome is oddly perverse. Nuclear power is now back in favour. The green movement activists think they have finally shifted the argument against the use of fossil fuels. They are right; we should be smarter than to destroy the planet just to make profit for a tiny minority. But the billions of pounds being sucked into nuclear power and the thousands of years of clean-up costs should bring everyone out in a cold sweat.

I had walked on the ridges west of Sheffield many years before when, on a clear day, it was easy to see a line of power stations in the far distance. It was cold so the 'cloud makers' were easy to spot. I pointed them out one by one to my then new partner, Caroline. Like some nerd I would tell her she could see ten gigawatts of coal-fired power in action as the water vapour rose above the eastern horizon. Not a chat-up line used by many others. The romance of power stations is not everybody's cup of tea and takes many years of practice. The sight of cooling towers in the distance revives the same old jokes.

With the industry in terminal decline the people of the coalfield areas did not disappear. Coal legacy issues rumbled on. Two of the main ones were: coal health compensation and miners' pensions.

The Labour government in its first term opened the door to two big ill-health compensation schemes. One covered what became loosely known as 'vibration white finger' and the second, a chest disease catch-all: 'chronic obstructive pulmonary disease' or COPD. A precursor to these schemes was the widespread claims for industrial deafness and the long-established pneumoconiosis scheme.

It was possible to get health compensation by taking individual cases to court and through what was the DHSS, but these two new waves of compensation were treated in effect as 'class actions'.

Hundreds of millions of pounds were channelled through these schemes to miners and ex-miners with health problems. Many people in the coalfield areas received significant compensation beneficial to families and the local economy. But then the law firms and companies involved in administration took a big slice as well. Some firms of solicitors charged a reasonable price, delivered a good service and were genuinely interested in righting old wrongs. Others milked the system.

Along with CCC colleagues, I attended liaison meetings with Department of Trade and Industry (DTI) civil servants to try to speed up the process and reduce spending on solicitors and administration. It was a legal quagmire and the feeding frenzy proved unstoppable.

The irony was that the money going to mining families was most probably recycled Treasury money taken out of the miners' pension funds.

When the industry was privatised the two main pension schemes were also handed over to private management. The Mineworkers Pension Fund (MPS) covered the weekly paid miners and the British Coal Staff Superannuation Scheme (BCSSS) covered salaried staff.[75] The schemes held billions of pounds of assets that in the stock market boom years had accumulated huge surpluses. Some of this was passed on to pensioners as bonuses and annual increases, but fifty per cent of it went to the Treasury under the terms of the agreement at the time of privatisation. The Treasury was the 'Guarantor' that pensions would never fall. This was a deal that no private sector fund could have struck, so at the time it seemed safe to stick with the government.

From 1994 until around 2016 some £8 billion was destined for the Treasury from surpluses. Although no government official would ever admit to it, this provided a handy source of income to cover coal industry legacy issues, including health compensation. I had sat in a meeting with a Secretary of State at DTI when a senior civil servant was forced to correct the Minister.

---

75 *Mineworkers Pension Scheme*, House of Commons Library Briefing. Annually updated.

In discussion, the Minister implied the pension surplus money was going back into coalfields through other channels. The civil servant stopped her in her tracks with a death stare. She was in the process of telling an unfortunate truth and was quickly and quietly silenced.

Campaigning to get more of the surpluses returned to mining pensioners began in earnest in 1999 and had some early success. The Government made £90 million available to top up the income of miners on very low pensions. The scheme for mineworkers was only begun in the 1970s, so miners with much of their service before then were on very small pensions.

Yet the bigger issue of the overall surpluses was not resolved. Fluctuations in the stock market and then the financial meltdown of 2007 onwards prevented any serious rethinking of the agreement put in place when the industry was privatised. Despite the uncertainties in the money markets, the funds remained in a strong position and the government has never paid a single penny into the schemes to cover the guarantee.

The coal industry itself had been used for decades to subsidise the energy costs of UK plc. The pension fund was a convenient and reliable source of income to cover some of the social costs as the industry passed into history.

Destroying the coal industry was the easy part. Resurrecting the economies and the social fabric of coalfield areas proved to be much harder. Thatcher had a plan to destroy the NUM but no plan for coalfield communities.

Successive government policies since the end of the strike in 1985 have appeared to be addressing coalfield 'regeneration', but the outcomes have fallen well short of the political rhetoric. For the best part of forty years since the need to 'regenerate' was first identified as an urgent priority, coalfield communities have remained some of the poorest areas in the UK. 'Levelling up' and 'building back better' may be the language of the Tories after 2019, but it's not new and not working.

It is not that nothing has been done – a host of initiatives and policies have been put in place over the years since mass closures. Some of these had genuine motivations and others were just political camouflage.

A Coalfield Task Force was set up in 1998 by the Blair government, and a number of its recommendations were implemented. This included the Coalfield Programme to restore derelict land, renew infrastructure and create new places of work. It also included the setting up of the Coalfields Regeneration Trust (CRT) to address unemployment and other social issues.

Support from European Union funding streams has helped to support any number of projects targeted at coalfield communities for twenty or more years. Many boxes have been ticked over those years and forms filled in, with some successes and lots of dead ends.

The stark reality is that coalfields, with some exceptions in the English Midlands, have not recovered and have not plugged into the economic prosperity seen elsewhere in the UK. They have changed significantly, but not always for the better. Precarious employment, under-employment and unemployment have become normalised. Politically the pendulum swung – Labour strongholds voting Tory for the first time ever in 2019. The Tory capture of the so-called 'Red Wall' constituencies became a source of angst for Labour and the left and endless analysis and re-analysis by commentators and academics.

My job with colleagues in the Coalfield Communities Campaign in all this was to articulate the needs of coalfield areas and persuade governments in London and Brussels to do more.

I regularly sat in meetings in Brussels with colleagues from other coalfield areas of Europe. The organisation was called EUR-ACOM (European Association of Coalfield Communities). It was made up of mainly EU member state groups but some of our most committed partners were from the Donbas coalfield of Ukraine and Rostov in Russia. At that time Eastern European partners believed the EU was the way forward. The British government perspective on this, needless to say, was deeply unhelpful. It should have come as no surprise that parking NATO tanks on Russian borders was never going to end well.

We all had a common cause, promoting policies and securing funding for areas trying to recover from mine closures. The EU was always sympathetic, even when the UK Government was often openly hostile – a cruel irony, given the anti-Europe sentiment so prevalent in English coalfield areas.

EU structural funds of various types found their way to the coalfields of the UK and propped up local economies for decades. Brexit propaganda distorted and twisted the views of all those who doubted government intentions in the past. This was a way out perhaps. Many people in the so-called 'Red Wall' areas bought the lies. The reality is that both the EU and the UK governments failed to support and re-build these local and regional economies. Abject failure all round, in most respects.

Despite the policy documents, and press releases and the ringing of hands, governments never did enough. There was never enough money, never enough effort, never enough imagination to tackle the huge problems. The austerity years of the Coalition, and then the Tory governments, eradicated any progress previously made using either EU or UK funding.

We at the Coalfield Communities Campaign became masters at complaining on behalf of under-funded local authorities. There was always so much evidence that could be deployed to demonstrate the problems, but that was not matched by workable solutions. Certainly not solutions that a deregulating, market forces-focused government might entertain.

Carrying a begging bowl was hardly edifying. Sitting in meetings, it was evident in the Minister's eyes:

"Oh, what is it that they want now? Why do these people think the world owes them a living? Why don't they disappear back up north and stop this tedious pestering?"

Barely tolerated by the hosts, delegations went home empty handed. Another day in London talking to people who must be seen to listen, but whose heads and hearts are elsewhere.

A former Chair of CCC tried to comfort me at one point by saying that without our efforts, things could have been even worse. Not getting your hopes up was the mantra as you got off the train in London.

In the last couple of years at work much of my time was spent defending employment in the UK steel industry. So many issues were much the same as those of coal and the lobbying and campaigning all so very familiar.

My working life had been transformed. No more squeezing through the bent steel bars in a crushed underground roadway in warm sticky air with a polished black face. No more painful scratches as coal and stone take little bites from bare flesh. No more spiralling coal dust whipping past. No more carefully removing the coal mascara from my sore eyes with Vaseline. No more chest x-rays in the back of a big blue and yellow van.

At CCC I spent the working day sitting at a computer; sitting on a train; sitting in the car; sitting in meetings. Ayrshire one day, the South Wales Valleys the next. Brussels next week and two London meetings on the way back. A small room with civil servants, maybe a Shadow Minister with an assistant or two, and even, but increasingly rarely, a Minister.

"Come in and sit down – very pleased to meet you."

Chairs scrape the floor, papers land on desks and everyone eyes each other up.

Introductions over, an outline of the problems and a shopping list are presented. The civil servants are in charge and skilfully obfuscate as the Minister tries to play the good guy.

"Well I have another appointment in fifteen minutes so … er … " The Minister is beginning to get bored.

A few hurried remarks if you can get them in and time's up, then handshakes and pleasantries. Afterwards, knowing looks and a post-meeting conflab in a coffee house on Victoria Street. Job done? Hardly.

"I need to phone the office," my boss informed me pulling out a ten-year-old mobile phone.

A minute or two later he confided, "That wasn't much help but we can dress it up as a partial success and try to be positive at next week's meeting in Torfaen. We will need to get the MPs' Group up to speed, so get on with it."

"Yes, right enough, I'll concentrate on the positives." My voice tails off.

Let me get on that soddin' train, I scream to myself. I've had enough of London for today!

It's then a clear week in the office trawling through other people's reports, writing your own reports and the endless exchange of emails. Team meetings, tricky phone calls, periods of boredom followed by frantic activity, giving the impression this is somehow really important. Staring at the walls looking for some inspiration to state the blindingly obvious in a new and interesting way. Failing to do so, I start chatting with a colleague. Well, that's another hour gone.

It's three in the afternoon and there is an energy dip. The brain has no spark at this time of day, so I resort to paper shuffling and hope not to get embroiled in anything urgent before five o'clock.

Next day it's up to Cumbria, a few well known friendly faces, handshakes, smiles, a presentation, local authority buffet – nothing much new. Then it's home, driving down the M6 and across the M62 on a Friday afternoon getting really cranked up as the queue of traffic backs up, two minutes of slow progress, stop, away again, slow, stop.

Marvellous, fantastic, the life of Riley, as they say. Talking to myself in the car is a bad sign I think – but it doesn't stop me. *I must try that mindfulness CD again …*

All a bit different to working for a living some might say. Yet the similarity with my former life is clear enough: I appear to be on the losing side again. Supporting Barnsley FC has its drawbacks too. Fighting lost causes, two steps forward and three steps back.

Look on the bright side, you don't have to get up at 4.30am and breathe in dust for hours on end. There is no need to jump out of your skin as a lump of stone flashes from the roof. The sheets on your side of the bed don't have that tell-tale grey sheen from coal dust migrating out of your skin in the night.

You have come to the end of your working life and spaces open up. Too often they feel like gaps not opportunities; time-lapse photography – long hours in the day and sometimes longer at night.

Making small decisions to do one thing or another seems to take on some significance but then you realise, there is no significance.

The days wash over you – some well spent, some wasted. You think the best is all behind you and then try to look forward to planned trips, time spent in the open air, on the hills, the wind in your face.

"The weather is fine today. You should make something of it", I tell myself.

The evening arrives. That wasn't so bad.

14

WALKING THIS ROAD TOGETHER – AND ALONE

A calm female voice: "Can I have your name and date of birth please?"

I mumble an answer but there is no one there to hear.

Then again: "Name and date of birth please … name and … name and …" The voice fades and disappears.

This is not a hospital ward I tell myself. Or is it?

Another of those dreams; another snippet of reality in with all the madness. Swirling, anxiety-filled fog, but no pit to go to thank the Lord!

It's morning again – another one. One eye open and some blurred shapes. The blackbird calls outside and the light comes through the curtains. No, it's not Firth 3.[76] Turning on my side and tucking my hands between my thighs, I curl up with my head under the covers. Eyes are tightly closed again.

It's not early and it's not dark, so what next? There's nothing to get up for. Well, I don't think so. I slap the pillow and shove it under my head a bit further. A few quiet grunts.

---

76 Firth 3 – a ward at Northern General Hospital, Sheffield.

This isn't going to work. I'll have to get up and make a cup of coffee.

And today is? I struggle for a second. What was yesterday? Then the minor events and activities of the past week pass through my mind in something like chronological order. I now at least know what day it is. I don't want to move but throw the duvet off and sit up staring across the bedroom then meander into the bog for a leak.

Staring into the bathroom mirror I am only too aware of how I have aged. At forty it felt like I was a thirty-year-old and at fifty like a forty-year-old. Now I feel and look my seventy years. People I knew years ago no longer recognise me. They can't see the mass of dark hair, so who is this bloke standing in front of them? I have had a serious health scare but was never unwell and my general fitness carried me through surgery and recovery. Yet my Peter Pan years are long gone.

Never comfortable looking in a mirror, I did not really want to know what I looked like or what I appeared like to the rest of the world. If I caught an image of myself in a mirror, I recoiled slightly. Hotel bedrooms had too many big mirrors and it was difficult to avoid yourself popping up from all angles.

It wasn't that there was much to avoid – nothing odd or repulsive – it was simply that such images reinforced the small inadequacies we all have and dents any confidence. The ears stuck out, there were now bags under the eyes, and of course, the mop of hair was now thin and grey. Was this aversion to mirrors just part of my vanity or evidence of my lack of vanity?

Why so much fuss about the way you look after all? Idiot! Get over it! More foolishness, more introspection, more niggling doubts.

Later in life the slowly advancing paunch was difficult to ignore – the trousers that were just a little bit too tight around the waist. As the years rolled on there was a surprise waiting: I realised that I had a look of my father. As a younger man I was convinced there was no resemblance. I did not look much like my brother or sister, so the genes must have had a good shake up at some point.

In my sixties the resemblance slowly emerged – a puzzled look, a frown, a quiet sigh, a pained expression of deep frustration that the world wasn't a better place. Short-fused and often irritable, I would more often than not, if given the choice by the nearest and dearest, shun company for a quiet life.

'Hell is other people' wasn't my phrase but I borrowed it from time to time. I had somehow turned into a version of my dad. We two men were well practised curmudgeons whose glass was always empty, so no chance it could ever be half full.

Growing old, some people would tell me, was a privilege. A privilege not given to everyone and not to those many people who were never allowed to grow old.

In my youth I soaked up the tales of the First World War fed by *The Great War Illustrated*, a leather-bound collection kept at my uncle's house. Loos, Verdun, the Somme, Ypres. Offensives, retreats, victories and defeats. Whatever these military actions were called, they all ended in some poor sods being blown to bits. A medal did little to stop the bleeding.

Wilfred Owen was on the school syllabus and the poetry stuck fast in the memory. Pat Barker brought it all back with her *Regeneration* trilogy many years later.

An English teacher introduced me to drama. As a sixth-former, I was in two plays: *Mother Courage and her Children* by Berthold Brecht, set in the Thirty Years War in central Europe, and *Oh What a Lovely War*, a satirical musical based on the contemporary songs of the World War One (Joan Littlewood's Theatre Workshop). The war theme was just reinforced.

We would visit my partner's grandad's grave in France – a little family pilgrimage that kept those dark days a second-hand memory. One hundred years after the end of the Great War, one hundred years since my partner's grandad was killed in action, I decided that was probably enough remembering.

Repeated on Armistice Day not long after 11am year after year, that extract from another poem was also very familiar to me:

'They shall not grow old, as we are left grow old:
Age shall not weary them, nor the years condemn'[77]

But I was not the 'doomed youth' of anthems, nor did I face any particular horrors. Count yourself lucky mate! Life, I was repeatedly told, was not fair.

---

77 *For the Fallen*: Laurence Binyon, 1914.

This was not based on some Zen mysticism, but merely the perceived experience of always having to kick up hill against a raging gale. Maybe I felt a little bit hard done to, but the sorrow was not for myself in the main. There is always so much to be disheartened about without dwelling on your own problems.

I am always saddened by the news of people who died without much of a life – young kids and babies in particular. The scenes captured on camera and broadcast the world over of kids being dragged from bombed buildings, were at the same time both naff caricatures and yet deeply troubling. A lump in the throat and a brief sigh.

On the television, famine and war stalked the earth as if Armageddon approached and then it was back to *Strictly Come Dancing*. It was impossible not to be moved, but then what could you do? Phone some number and give them twenty quid, apparently.

Children carry such a weight of responsibility, poor little things. They need to be healthy, to cry and smile in equal measure, but above all, to live as long as possible. Old people die eventually – young people live … isn't that the way of it? Seems not.

I remember Kate, my eldest daughter, had a miscarriage before going on to have two girls. It was fairly early in the pregnancy so I assumed it was not too traumatic. These things happen and life goes on, I thought. How wrong could I be? The crushed and inconsolable look on my daughter's face took me aback. Sad dark eyes; such pain and sadness in one so dear. Life and death in one very short episode.

It wasn't that I was somehow obsessed with death, far from it. I was spared any personal tragedy for much of my adult life. My parents lived to be old – my mother into her nineties.

My partner's brother was not so fortunate. He died when he was fifty of a brain tumour. His struggle over many months was so very hard and cast a dark shadow over the wider family. There was little that could be done, but that did not stop Caroline trying. She moved heaven and earth to do her best for her dear brother.

But lives cut short in the coal mines were the tragedies that were filed away in my mind and rarely forgotten. The long history of carnage faced by coal miners was very close to home. Lives snuffed out below ground, blown to bits, lungs burnt to cinders or quietly suffocated. Little gasps of air slowing and becoming shallower. People torn limb from limb by heartless machinery and men dying early from lung disease. I could not erase the knowledge of families left destitute beyond mourning, living out lives stripped of hope, some held together by strong women, others forlorn and lost in a huge sea of 'have nots' whose histories are perhaps 'known unto God' – but few others. This was part of my history as much as theirs.

"You're a long time dead," pit work mates would tell me. This mind-numbing thought was supposed to encourage you to live in the present and take adversity in your stride. It served mainly to remind me, as I reached my seventies, that many of those same mates were already dead. A roll call that was getting longer.

Tony, my long-time mucker in the coal face team, died way back in 2010. He was the machine man and I was the 'snaker', two peas in a pod. We ripped the piss out of each other but there was a common bond, with no bad feelings.

When he died, I was in Hampshire at a funeral – one of Caroline's relatives. I arrived home just before Christmas and picked up emails, and whatever else I'd missed. There it was: a message about his funeral. I sat staring into the mid-distance. We did not keep in touch, but the truth was, it was me who did not keep in touch with him. There were to be more and more such regrets, so many missed opportunities to say farewell to old workmates.

The circle has been broken and the lives and deaths of thousands of miners and their families are now only of curious historical interest. Nostalgia, myth and wonder replace the reality of early mornings, hard work, noise and dust. The countless dead from accidents and disease provide a vast audience looking on all knowingly. A vast choir but with no voice.

In the year 1931, when my dad first went down the mines, there were 869 fatalities. The year of the disaster involving my uncle, there were 802 killed in the coal mines. By nationalisation in 1947, this had fallen to 618. When I first went down the pit in 1977, the death toll was 48.

Reflections often ended up somewhere near my parents' gravestone. Only a few yards away, a Celtic Cross marks the grave of my great grandfather and great grandmother. The grass is cut, but not that often it seems. Perhaps graveyards look better a little shabby. A cemetery with many Welsh names, but more unmarked graves unnoticed.

The ghosts of the Welsh diaspora somewhere under the trees and in the hedgerows. Immigrants and outsiders speaking a different language perhaps to some. But we are all immigrants from somewhere if we go back far enough. All incomers, all 'blow-ins' from other places. Coal mines and coal communities were often populated with people of many backgrounds. Some desperate and living on the margins eking out a life in whatever way they could. My family on the other hand were bastions of the local community until the depression took its toll. Now most of this is long forgotten.

Coal mines had seen great wealth created for some individuals. Coal had also benefitted the whole country, going back two hundred years or more. The industrial revolution and the British Empire were built on coal.[78]

"It all comes off the shovel", the pit lads would say as they stared at country mansions.

The mines had seen more sorrow than joy and the 1936 disaster at Wharncliffe Woodmoor colliery was just one of many major accidents that snuffed out lives and left further poverty in their wake. But it was a disaster so close to home for me. It was my history. My uncle inspected the scene underground after the explosion and was called to give evidence at the Inquiry. My father was on the other shift.

Not one word was exchanged between me and father about the deaths of the fifty-eight men. Yet, decades later in that small envelope tucked away with the insurance policies and family paperwork were handwritten notes and memos from management just hours prior to the explosion. Artefacts from a bygone age. No explanation will ever be forthcoming.

Father wasn't big on explanations or idle tittle-tattle and his true nature was bit of a mystery to us kids.

Anecdotally, I was to learn my father was considered a 'dry' bloke with a sharp

---

78 Jeremy Paxman, Black Gold. 2021.

and sometimes dark sense of humour. This was not the father who sat at home occasionally making scathing comments about the government or Coal Board. He was animated by matters I did not then understand. Alf Robens, the former Chairman of the Board, was the devil incarnate in our house, having shut many pits in the late fifties and sixties. My father had worked at four pits in the area from 1933 onwards. Pit closures weren't invented by Margaret Thatcher.

Father was a regular worker and never 'knocked' shifts on Monday morning or Friday night as many colliers did. He even turned up on his last day of work after forty-eight straight years down the pit. Management shook their heads, smiled and sent him home. He may have been well known to any number of pitmen in the area but not really known to his children.

For me, Dad always had a defeated air about him. Years of shift work, not surprisingly, did nothing to cheer up his disposition – or that is how I chose to interpret it. Being quiet and withdrawn in company was my father's way. When we were kids he would occasionally start to sing some song from an old film. There was some joy in there somewhere.

In his final years, when dementia took hold, it was sometimes difficult to gauge his state of mind – there was not much to go on from conversation. He would sit in a corner when the family turned up with grandkids in tow. A little smile and a faraway look in his eye, but not much to say.

He could easily get grumpy and occasionally very agitated but not in the company of his family. My mother took the brunt of the moods. I took my father's repressed anger and frustration to be a result of being a defeated old bloke with nothing much to show for a lifetime down the pit.

Unlike his fellow workers in the 1936 disaster, age did weary him and the years condemned him. He had survived all that hard pit work could throw at him, but died in a hospital ward drugged up with morphine. Dad had always said, "Well at least I'll not end up in the workhouse … " By a sneaky twist of fate, that cathedral-like hospital ward in which he passed his last moments was converted from Fir Vale Workhouse some decades before. *Sorry Dad – didn't see that one coming.*

Once again it was in the act of trying to clear up a lifetime of junk in cupboards and under beds, I came across some more scribblings I had made at the time of Dad's death.

The notes I made appear to be me trying to straighten out my own mind about what had happened – my role, the family's role and the role of the NHS and care homes. At the time I was very angry and looking to apportion blame, or at least find some logic to a situation that deteriorated out of control in the last weeks and months of Dad's life.

Accumulation of problems resulted in a crisis when this millennium was but a few hours old. Dad did a runner. He disappeared into the night and was found in the early hours by police – cold, dazed and confused.

Mother was not sure when he left, she only knew he was making a grand gesture by leaving her and going back home to his mother in the next village, some two miles away. He may have had suicide on his mind.

The family did not know the extent of his dementia until the chaotic hours of 2 January 2000. Mother must have – but she never said. His doctor must have – but he never said.

Watching the police helicopter overhead brought me to my senses like a shot from a gun. Would anyone ever be happy again?

Did he have money with him? Would he take off his boots, tuck the money inside, and jump in the canal? (A tale told many years before.)

Dad was found and taken to Barnsley General Hospital. He was very cold but mercifully the elements had been kind and the night was mild for January.

"Can you tell me the name of the Queen of England?" asked the doctor.

Dad turned to me – "What's he on about?" He asked, puzzled by this quiz game.

"Who is the Prime Minister?" Continued the doctor earnestly.

"Well I know it's not Gladstone or Disraeli … it's that young bloke," replied father,

smirking mischievously.

The family had to face up to the brutal truth that Dad would never go home and needed specialist care. It was no use pretending otherwise, but the guilt was still there, burrowing deep.

Abandoning your parents to an institution feels like a betrayal.

Nothing really worked out or went to plan. Dad was restless and sometimes aggressive with carers and other old people alike. It was his revenge for being dumped with a bunch of strangers.

Problems were reported directly to the family on the phone as though we could do anything about it.

I am told – "He has thrown a wobbler and dragged an old lady out of her room" (I am thinking – he thought it was his room – the rooms all look alike).

"He has broken the furniture in his room!"

As a result, he was referred to a psychiatrist and put on a drugs regime.

It was obvious the drugs were having a bad effect. He became lethargic and immobile – slowly turning into a zombie.

After a collapse he is taken to hospital. No doubt the care home breathed a sigh of relief having got rid of the troublesome old bugger.

He doesn't give in and is once again disruptive. More heavy drugs are used and the man is "poleaxed" – a consultant's words, not ours.

The family try a rescue but, despite visiting any number of care homes, no one really wants him in that state.

A phone call at some god-awful hour. I murmur, "They've killed him – they have killed him."

But not yet, as it turned out.

Dad died at 7.55am on 30 October, 2000. Cause of death on the certificate was pneumonia with contributing factor of a stroke or strokes (transient ischemic attacks).

Neil, Mam and I sit out the final hours. We are told that medical intervention was possible but not advised. Dad lay on the bed eyes shut and gasping for air. The doctor returned and said he wanted to administer diamorphine to make him more comfortable.

Lamely I say. "OK … but not too much." What on earth was I thinking – assisting in the death?

After a while the old man seemed to settle and his breathing became steadier. For one fleeting moment I thought maybe he might just get through this. But the breathing became shallower and then less frequent.

Slowly he began to shut down. Little breaths misting up his transparent mask. As the leaves blew off the trees through the window on this stormy night, the light began to build. He ebbed away.

A nurse was summoned and she confirmed it was near the end.

"Go to sleep now, it's all over," she whispered in his ear.

Ominously, my notes go on to say:

The circumstances that led to his death and the process he was put through need to be questioned.

But they never were. It was a rant. I realised it was mainly my actions, or lack of them, that really bothered me. I could not apportion blame if I too was at fault. Was there more that could have been done? That being said, the care home did not do much caring and the whole system was, and still is, a national disgrace, an indictment on a so-called 'civilised society'.

At Dad's funeral in the chapel, just yards from the small house where we had lived briefly with grandmother and Uncle Richard, I stood in the pulpit and reflected on my father's life. Some of the Welsh diaspora attended having been informed by the Minister. They perhaps knew Father rather better than his children ever did.

My ageing aunt remarked with pride that her nephew had "taken the lesson" at the chapel. The thought of me standing there in a dog-collar pontificating about life, death and immortality was amusing. A leftie atheist perhaps – I considered myself to have a spiritual side and was happy to embrace the good in any religion.

The speech was not long. A thank you or two, then back to a potted history:

It is ironic, but at the same time fitting, that he should have passed away at the beginning of the new century, a new millennium.

He and people like him were very much part of the last century …

Forty-eight years a miner spent under the very ground we now stand on …

I dare say he would have chosen a different kind of life if there had been any option, but for kids growing up around here in the twenties and thirties there was no choice.

Just as the coal industry is now confined to history, so are most of the many, many thousands of people who work in it …

We have brought you back here to be with your mother and father, in familiar surroundings and with fond memories. Take a long rest now – you have earned it!

It was the same streets, the working men's club and the racing pigeons in flight. The scene where we paid those visits to Uncle Richard in the fifties had changed, but not much. The pit tip was now rounded off with a covering of rough grass, lame bushes and grey bare patches. A less than convincing attempt to return it to nature.

Nearby was the memorial to the fifty-eight men who were killed in 1936. A lasting memorial and a place in the history books was theirs to own.

An unknown bit of history was to be found elsewhere. A first-hand record hidden in an old envelope smeared with coal dust, but real memories long buried. Scraps of paper barely recognisable, yet reflections on people taken violently away – Body 'A', Body 'B', Body 'C', Body 'D' – recorded for ever in scruffy pencil. Bare, minimal facts – no emotion, no background story, no faces of the mourning, no tears from loved ones.

Some years later I found myself addressing another gathering of friends and relatives at my mother's funeral. As with my father, I tried to make the story of her life interesting and eventful. But her life too was ordinary and largely unremarkable. Bringing up three kids and working to pay the bills did not leave too much time for great deeds or public acclaim.

The high point for her was in the Women's Auxiliary Air Force during the Second World War. You could not take that away from her. She had the medals to prove it. "Bomber Command!" I joked, ribbing her about her role in flattening Germany. "What about Dresden? The indiscriminate bombing of civilians? Any ideas about that?" I taunted. She would not be drawn.

Her job in the war was repairing barrage balloons in East Yorkshire, defending Hull and its docks. Hull was subjected to repeated air raids. When the Luftwaffe threat receded, she ended up working in the camp Post Office. Her conversations came to life talking about those days in the war – "in the forces" as she would say, recalling her exploits. It was a time when she had a role, she was appreciated and given self-worth. Bringing up three kids in a small terrace house gave her little to cheer about.

After demobilisation she was a clippy[79] on the buses in Barnsley. Yorkshire Traction was the local bus company – such a splendid name and evocative

---

79 Bus conductor with a ticket machine slung over neck and shoulder.

of another era. She is said to have met my dad on one of these noisy red double-deckers.

Most of her working life was in clothing factories that clustered in many mining communities. This work too has largely gone the way of other traditional employment.

She was a skilled machinist and was utterly wasted repeatedly sewing cuffs and collars to countless shirts. She changed jobs many times. She was confident in her own abilities and value to the rag trade and refused to compromise. If she was not allowed to do a first-class job and told to put speed first rather than quality, she did not want the job. A National Union of Tailors and Garment Workers badge on her overcoat.

She slipped away without a murmur at breakfast one day. No drama, just another old lady in a care home passing her last breath slumped in front of a cup of tea. Her ashes too are now in the same cemetery we knew so well as children.

The uttered words filled the spaces between me and the assembled people but then were lost. Going through the motions and doing what was expected, I soldiered on. The sixties' architecture of the crematorium chapel more reminiscent of school than any house of God.

The reflections were modest, kind and well-meaning, but fleeting and intangible. Coming into this world alone and leaving alone. The last judgment? Hardly, hardly much at all. Just a few words from a grieving son trying to hide my regrets, trying to pass on a little bit of the love for the last time. What more could we have done to mark her passing?

There were some sad looks as I peered over the reading glasses. Faces tight-lipped and some distant. With the odd glance to the heavens in front of me, I managed to stay composed. Was anybody weeping? I was not. The voice wavered for a moment, then I drew breath and recovered.

The celebrant finished her words and it was over. We all filed out slowly down a corridor into the open air, now free to chat. The order and required serenity of the funeral service came swiftly to an end and a buzz of conversation built up. "Long time no see … Are you keeping well?" is a good place to start in such conversations.

In late December 2015 people assembled for a demonstration and rally in Knottingley, near Pontefract, West Yorkshire. Kellingley Colliery was across the river and the canal looking much like it always had.

Pit banners unfurled in the winter breeze, familiar faces, nods of recognition from those who had trod the streets of pit towns for many years. Women Against Pit Closures, Jobs Not Jail, Orgreave Truth and Justice – back together in common cause.

A few brown leaves still cling stubbornly to the trees lit by the low sun. A band starts up then stops and some discordant brass instrument tails off and it's quiet again, except for a background drone of traffic on the main road.

It was as if nothing had changed. The paraphernalia of miners' demonstrations much the same. But it had changed so very much.

"Is Joe still with us?" A stout, red-faced man asks.

"No, he died last year. Not many of us left it seems … " came the matter of fact reply.

"Ken?"

"I never see Ken any more. He is always at his caravan in Skeggy."

"And Alf?"

"Do you know it must be fifteen years since I saw him – no idea what became of him. You'd hear him first before you saw him!"

A few more names and few more questions about their whereabouts and the conversation stops abruptly when a brass band starts up and then just as quickly stops again.

The truth was, I had lost touch with most of my old workmates. I may have worked with them but I did not live in their company. I didn't spend much time in pit villages anymore. A slow process of de-coupling over the years was leaving bigger and bigger gaps.

"Who is that bloke over there? I know his face but can't for the life of me remember the name." I start running through the alphabet to give my brain a jolt. No, it's not working, I can't recall the name. Little scenes appear in the mind's eye, like long-lost videos in the recesses of the brain.

"Do you remember when the overman, Tommy – er Tommy – no can't remember his second name. Anyway, he got hit with a rock fall on the face side? The deputy wrote '*Rock on Tommy*' on the accident report." There is a little snigger from the two of them.

"And then when Dunk was refused new pit boots on Friday nightshift and you had to come to the pit to prevent a strike?"

"No, wasn't me. I didn't come, I'd had a skinful of ale – it was 9.30 on Friday evening. I was driving nowhere. It was one of the Branch Officials from the village who walked up to sort it out."

Tales of 'the old days' pass between the gathered people and looking to the future is generally avoided.

There's so much to remember, so much hidden in the back of the mind that defies all efforts to recall. Events merge and the sequence is often lost. Thinking back there are so many gaps but then, does it matter so much? Some snatches of memories unconnected – others etched deep in his mind. Sights, sounds and smells evoking something, but I am not always sure what.

The last deep mine in the UK – Kellingley – had just closed. There was plenty of media coverage, but no real battle to save it. Resignation and memories. Nostalgia once again reigns. There is no call-to-arms, no appeals for support, no fists raised in anger or even despair.

This brought to an end centuries of coal mining in Britain.

It was another funeral of sorts, but it wasn't a person that had died; it was an industry, a way of life and once thriving communities. There were no tears, but plenty of lumps in the throat as the industry was laid to rest. A few beers in the pit club put the seal on it and people dispersed to continue their own stories of miners and mining. Or perhaps they didn't anymore.

A poster with the NUM badges of all the closed pits had been produced many years earlier by former Nottinghamshire strikers and proudly stated:

People will always need coal – Time the Avenger!

But it seems no one needs coal. Time avenges, yes – but we are all its victims.

Once again, the heroic optimism of an earlier time brings wry smiles to ex-miners and former mining communities the length and breadth of the country. Government promotions and National Coal Board recruitment propaganda of the 1950s and 60s about Britain's future strength coming from coal appear now to be a sick joke.

As an ex-miner, NUM activist and campaigner for regeneration and 'levelling up' of mining communities for most of my working, and then retired life – the biggest knock-back in recent years was the result of the December 2019 general election. I was used to the drip, drip, drip of adversity, but events conspired to knock my duck completely off.

Personal loss of friends and family are all part of life. Yet for someone who always expected that the world and its people would move, however unsurely, towards a better world – I looked around in despair.

Much of the non-metropolitan working class had come to the conclusion over years of neglect that successive governments were pissing up their backs. Sticking to the piss metaphor – as they may have said to the political elite of the prosperous South East: "Don't piss on my boots and tell me it's raining!"

Brexit was the chosen weapon of dissent – despite its right wing and often racist connections. The trade union movement was a shadow of its former self and the Labour party had been losing support over the decades of industrial decline. Good jobs were in short supply – shit jobs were plentiful.

Revived by hopes that Jeremy Corbyn might shift the Labour Party back to its socialist principles, I and many others worked hard to elect them in two successive general elections. I shared many of Corbyn's political views but I was never convinced he was Prime Minister material. An MP and Party leader who was an old, white, middle-class bloke from London, ticked no boxes. Still the manifesto was a great improvement on the Blair years. "Nothing to lose," I thought. Yes – I was wrong, and not for the first or last time.

Starmer, yet another white bloke from the metropolitan elite, looked a possibility, but in truth there wasn't much competition. At first, he sounded like someone who grasped some notion of socialism. It did not last long and he was captured by the faceless machine that undermined Corbyn and that often drives Labour. A machine so clearly exposed by the Forde Report[80]. This 'get politics out of politics' faction born in the Blair years appeal to the establishment and anybody prepared to stick their cross on a ballot paper. Invade the Middle East to support an idiot in the White House? Why not? Equality and fairness never on the agenda.

The election campaign of 2017 seemed to indicate things were going in the right direction but it proved a false dawn and wishful thinking for so many committed lefties. The December 2019 General Election need never have happened, but happen it did.

It is difficult to get a sound overview when you are tramping the streets knocking on doors and hoping for a friendly reception. The signs were not good. Apparently Corbyn was an IRA supporter, at least people on the doorstep thought so. He was a 'communist' they said – as if this was an insult. "No more left wing than Harold Wilson," I suggested. I never bothered to tell them that the IRA had sound reasons for resisting British occupation and communism had got a bad name mainly because of Joe Stalin and similar autocrats. The basic principles of communism were equality and fairness. I was reluctant to engage at this level because I did not want to come over as another 'loony' leftie. I had tried for many years to adhere to my 'credible left' label.

I only wanted an answer to one question from the people I have met when discussing politics: "Whose side are you on?" I am not particularly interested in the tedious debates so common on the left. A newspaper article, probably in *The Guardian*, once described the British left as "boring as door knobs!" Yes, I get it, but at least you can open a door with a door knob.

In the difficult Penistone and Stocksbridge constituency north of Sheffield in the campaign I was confronted by a strange verbal assault. A knock at the door and a woman opened it.

"We are canvassing on behalf of the Labour candidate. Are there any particular issues you think are important?" This stuff just trips off the tongue.

A bloke ran down the stairs, ordered his wife into the kitchen and proceeded to threaten me. He had a fishing reel in his hands but I never got the chance to ask about his sporting achievements. My daughter and friend

---

80 Labour Party, *Forde Report*, July 2022.

were also canvassing and stopped to witness the fracas. The man's eyes bulged even more.

"Oh! I fucking see now: a bunch of gender-bending snowflakes. Just fuck off before a I slot you!"

"Take the first swing if you want, bud," I informed him, trying very hard not to lose my temper. As a kid and young man I never ran away from a fight, but did not win many either.

"Oh yes, what are you going to do about it?" he continued, walking towards me.

Being in effect a representative for the Labour Party I counted to ten and walked away. I resisted the temptation to suggest to his wife that she phone Women's Aid.

I barely knew the meaning of the insults and could not fathom the depth of hate he appeared to have for me. Not reading the *Sun* or *Daily Star*, I had missed out on understanding a whole section of the population and was left puzzled and alarmed that this general election was going to be a train crash for Labour.

The election campaign was intense and I rarely stood back to make an honest assessment. There are always unpleasant people knocking about and there are lots of people who don't seem to give a toss one way or another – so who's counting?

Spreading myself across all the local seats with problems for Labour, I inevitably ended up in the pit village where I worked for fifteen years. I was expected to take advantage perhaps of old associations. But I had barely set foot in the village for twenty years at least, so I had no high hopes. The outgoing Labour MP had been elected for decades with little opposition. He was a former miner and NUM official from Maltby, so I knew him of old. The new Labour candidate was young and had no track record in the area.

True enough, the reception was underwhelming but, thankfully, no headcases greeted me on the doorstep. It was, in fact, worse.

An ex-miner I knew from the neighbouring pit smiled – he was pleased to see Labour were making an effort but he warned me I was on a hiding to nothing. It was not the same anymore – trade unionism was as good as dead and no one gave a shit about anything. On top of that, the media destruction of Jeremy Corbyn had been swallowed hook, line and sinker.

I knocked on another door. A dishevelled bloke opened it and I instantly recognised him as an electrician from my former pit. He helped me out with his name. He knew mine, after all I was the NUM delegate of yesteryear and I even tried to buy the pit to keep good jobs in the village.

"Where have *you* been for the last twenty odd years? You're a bit late aren't you? Sorry, you are wasting your time and mine. I'm voting Conservative – your lot have done nothing. I know my dad would turn in his grave if he knew, but that's as may be. Shut the garden gate when you leave."

"OK. I get the message. Look after yourself," I managed to reply and walked off. By coincidence this was the same street I had been set upon by a senior police officer with his mates in blue back in the strike. So much had changed and I was out of touch. But then so was the Labour Party. Knocking on doors with promises that are never delivered was not going to change much. If this was coming full circle, I had not expected it.

The calamity of the December 2019 general election is for others to analyse in detail. So too is the loss of the 'Red Wall' to the Tories and the many convoluted explanations that continue to exercise the minds and column inches of both left and right. For now, I will stick with the succinct and clear message from that former miner on his doorstep. Where indeed had I been? "You only come around here when you want our votes!" is a well-worn sentiment and usually a fair criticism.

That December, a day or so after the general election a close friend and neighbour of mine dropped dead of a heart attack. He loved his hills and he loved his politics. He died on his own, in his flat, no one to help. I could not blame this on Boris Johnson or any other Tory from Ted Heath to Liz Truss. Most of the shit in the UK could be laid at their door – but not everything. This loss set the tone.

Deaths and funerals punctuate your life and the reflections on what might have been intensify. Introspection tends to fill the empty moments. It cannot be helped. Disaster comes in many forms – Wharncliffe Woodmoor 1936, Spanish Civil War 1936, Munich 1958, Aberfan 1966, Miners' Strike 1984–85, Hillsborough 1989, end of the UK coal industry 2015, Grenfell Tower 2017.

Thankfully, the quiet death of an old woman stirs different emotions. After the proceedings at my mother's funeral, I walked back to the car almost empty of thoughts or emotions. The body mechanically obeying orders. Mirror – signal – manoeuvre. A long stare at the sky, but nothing registers. A gaze at my shoes to avoid any eyes. Eyes always hit the target. They search and tell, and pierce the hardest human armour. With or without mirrors, with or without remorse. The eyes will always reveal the truth.

Like all funerals, there is a bit of a 'do' at the house. The family comes together now – it doesn't happen that often. My family were never close. There is no open expression of emotions one way or another. Relatives and friends stand around in the downstairs rooms. There is plenty of chat and catching up to do. But the pressure is off. This chapter is over.

In my mind I am drawn to the mirror once again. So many reflections, some clear images, some blurred and also so many distortions, so many versions of the truth. The reflections of many others will follow.

A short while later and only the close family remain. Head in hands, but not in sorrow, I stare into the middle distance, I search for some inspiration. No mirror interrupting my vacant view. What now am I looking for? What now can be waiting for me?

Current time seems to pass very slowly, yet decades have slipped by and old age creeps up.

Nature replenishes me if nothing much else helps. The birds around the house give me some comfort. A blackbird on the neighbours' old TV aerial is singing its little heart out. A wren flits about in the hedges. The goldfinches are busy and that nuthatch keeps turning up to brighten my day. It's spring again and my mood shifts a little.

"How are you feeling?" many people ask.

"Oh – you know – fair-to-middling, up and down," I might reply.

Memories are now a little kinder and easier to manage. The grand plans, the upper reaches of ambition seem mistaken, misjudged. Yet more doubt, more soul searching. Relax man! Who am I to sit and feel so sorry for myself? Age has wearied me but I am better off than most and tragedy has not waylaid me yet.

You are indeed a long time dead.

○ ○ ○

I cast my mind back to my mining days with all the laughs and the tears. Many of the reflections are indistinct and out of sequence. Nostalgia, half-truths and myths fill in some of the gaps. For some it's perhaps hard to believe any of it ever existed. I am one of many thousands still around to tell the tale. But for how long?

I rarely returned to the pit village where I worked nor the one I was brought up in. Regret and guilt haunt me as a result. I am very aware of all the good things about pit villages, but my personal history and relationship is complex. Love and admiration are part of the picture, but so is exasperation.

Nevertheless, I found myself going back to my pit site many years after the closure. The pit tip, crudely landscaped, provided a rolling backdrop as life carries on. Dog walkers and retired miners with nothing much else to do, wander around the scrubby landscape. Racing pigeons once again flying in formation, bank and dive over the open ground, their feathers reflecting back the low sun.

No flurry of activity at shift change-over times. No pit hooter. No trains clanking slowly up and down the single-track branch line and no lorries queuing to be loaded with coal. No little whirlwinds of grey dust up the pit lane. But here the sun rises and sets like everywhere else and people have the same needs and aspirations as they always had. Forgotten by the powers that be, they carry on.

There is a new business estate on the neighbouring pit site, but not here. This is a dormitory village, but not a fashionable place to live with its mix of mainly former council or pit houses. Gentrification will not happen here. Most jobs are some miles away. Many other pit sites were developed for warehouse and distribution centres. Massive huts enslaving a younger generation in mindless low paid drudgery.

A memorial obelisk stands in a garden of remembrance to all those who were killed at the pit. The NUM banner is a hung in a local church. Hopefully somethings will outlast this generation and stand the test of time.

Some pubs have been demolished, but the pit club survives. The village moves on. People move on and new people move in. It is difficult to see just how the village can find a new role or generate any prosperity. There are some people who will at least try. For many of the miners who worked at the pit, the redundancy pay-out soon went and other jobs were hard to find. Industrial injury compensation and disability payments helped but didn't build a future. As old age and illness took their toll the collective memory is slowly erased.

Time alone will tell if there is better to come for the younger generation or just a slow decline, a steady wearing down of hopes and expectations.

It was, and in many ways still is, a pit village – but that too will fade. Trade union solidarity and Labour sentiments weakening relentlessly as the Thatcher years morphed into those of Blair and then years of austerity. For the first time ever, in December 2019 the constituency returned a Tory MP. Political pundits in the media and intellectuals on the left are still trying to work that one out. For now – I will leave them to it.

'Levelling up' in this village has always been no more than an empty soundbite. Successive governments have let these places down. There is not much scope for optimism, but we are obliged to try to remain hopeful for future generations in all former coalfield communities.

Coalface. Acrylic on canvas. © David J Parry.

POSTSCRIPT

This life I have lived has always straddled class divisions. A great grandfather who was manager of a colliery; a father who spent all his working life working down coal mines; a son (me) who, having passed his 11-plus exam, ended up as the first member of the immediate family with a university degree, but then after, the last-but-one member of the family to work down a coal mine. Neil, my brother, was the last.

Riven with inarticulate and emotional contradictions, the decades passed. An unremarkable existence. No drama, no outward anguish – just background tensions. Noises off. A young man with some zeal to change the world. A middle-aged man with expectations of progress for humanity. Thwarted it seems for now.

Political, social and cultural developments, such as the re- emergence of right-wing populism and the retreat of the trade union and Labour movement, bring the background tensions to the fore. Not so easy now to look the other way. Hopes and expectations turn easily to dismay and not a little anger.

The resurgence of trade union activity in 2022 and 2023 suggest all is not lost.

The world has changed faster than an ageing bloke can keep up with. Looking once again at that reflection in the mirror does not help. All you see are your own shortcomings. Still waiting? Still grasping at straws? Tomorrow, no doubt, will be a better day.

Wash Day Blues

The soap is white
Water hot and colourless
Now an armful of clothes from the basket
Pushed deep into the water
Black scum rises slowly to the surface
Then bubbles

Grey water gently swirling in the tub
Thrashing now
A bead of sweat on her brow
The bubbles fight for dear life
Back and forth, up and down
Twisted clothes give up their grime

All at rest beneath the surface
A truce, a ceasefire, flat calm
The air is streaked with wisps of steam
Maybe now it's nearly all over
In the steam a smell – one smell
The smell of soap and coal

By the author.

Two seven five

Arms outstretched he pushed down the button
A flash of light plays across his closed eyelids
Awake – but only just – he throws back covers
Sitting up he swivels and bare feet touch the carpet
Move man! Move – you know the routine

Another button results in boiling water
Instant coffee is as good at it gets
Bread, hard cold butter and some cheese
Bread bag – wrapped and nestling in his coat pocket
Car keys? House keys? Cash? Door

The street and the iced-up car glisten under the orange light
Scraping the screen – this way then that – engine ticking over
Empty world, wisps of fog and frost shimmering roads
Pit yard and bright spotlights silhouette hunched figures
Head down through the comers and goers

He arrives at a little window to a familiar face
"Two seven five" – the only words needed
Brass in hand he steps into the neon strip lights
The banging of locker doors greets him again
That same old smell – coal and soap

By the author.

On Firth Three

On Firth Three the lights stayed on
Daylight comes but not here
A glance over the shoulder says different
That bloke in the white coat is changing sheets
One step at a time

Diagnosis, prognosis, neurosis
A dark cloud moves slowly across the mind
Nothing hurts so nothing to worry about
Cut morphine I am told
Sounds good to me pal

Looking around you meet up with eyes
Knowing eyes or so they think
It's not their fault no more than yours
It's how it is on Firth Three
Waiting now for the next long, long night

By the author.

Tears and Fears

Weep my friend and weep again
No shame in weeping
Weeping stops the bastards getting to you

Not weeping lets the bastards in
So weep some more
Until you settle on a plan

The plan is to weep

Weep when you feel like it
Weep when there is no option
Weep and then stop

Nobody likes a cry baby

By the author.

GLOSSARY

Air dowors	Doors erected to provide a ventilation circuit
Banksman	Worker at top of shaft – signalling to winder
CH4	Methane
Chocker(s)	Operator(s) of face supports
Chocks	Multi legged, hydraulic supports
COSA	Colliery Overmen and Staff Area
Cowl	Semi-circular plough on a coal cutting disc
Deputy	Official on each underground district
Developments/headings	Tunnelling roadways to open up new faces
Dint	Mining the floor beneath a seam
Dosco Dintheader	Heading machine usually for in-seam mining
Downcast	Shaft taking air into the mine
Dowty prop	Manually operated hydraulic pit prop
Face market	Pool of face workers to cover absentees
Flight bars	Steel cross bars between chain on panzer/stage loader
Gob	Waste or fallen ground at back of a face
Haigh Moor, Swallow Wood etc.	Names of seams of coal
Inbye	Furthest workings in any given area e.g. face or heading
m/c	machine
Main gate (Loader gate)	Intake air to/coal conveyor from a face
NACODS	National Association of Colliery Overmen, Deputies and Shot-firers
NCB	National Coal Board
Number 1 machine	The main coal cutting machine on a face – shearer
Oldham/Aldwarke/Garforth	Types of safety lamp
Onsetter	Worker at bottom of shaft – signalling to winder
Ops Manager	Operations Manager from Area in charge of a number of pits
Outbye	Workings away from faces and headings nearer pit bottom
Packhole(s)	Support to gate side at each end of a face
Paddy	Underground man-riding train
Pan/pan line	Sections of armoured flexible conveyor
Panel	NUM organisation relating to NCB areas in Yorkshire
Panzer	Armoured flexible face conveyor
Rip	Mining the roof above a seam to form a roadway
Rippers	Workers advancing roadway behind/in line with a face
S01s, H02s etc.	Names of particular faces or underground districts
Snaker	A miner who hydraulically advances face conveyor and supports
Snap time	Twenty minutes break in a shift for a snack
Stable hole	Area mined at each end of face to allow machine to advance into new cut
Stage loader	Armoured conveyor in roadway
Stone dust	Form of limestone dust used to help suppress fires/explosions etc.
Tail gate (Supply gate)	Return air and supply roadway to a face
Transport rules	Management rules for underground transport – signal codes etc.
UDM	Union of Democratic Mineworkers
Upcast	Shaft for return air (usually with the main fan)

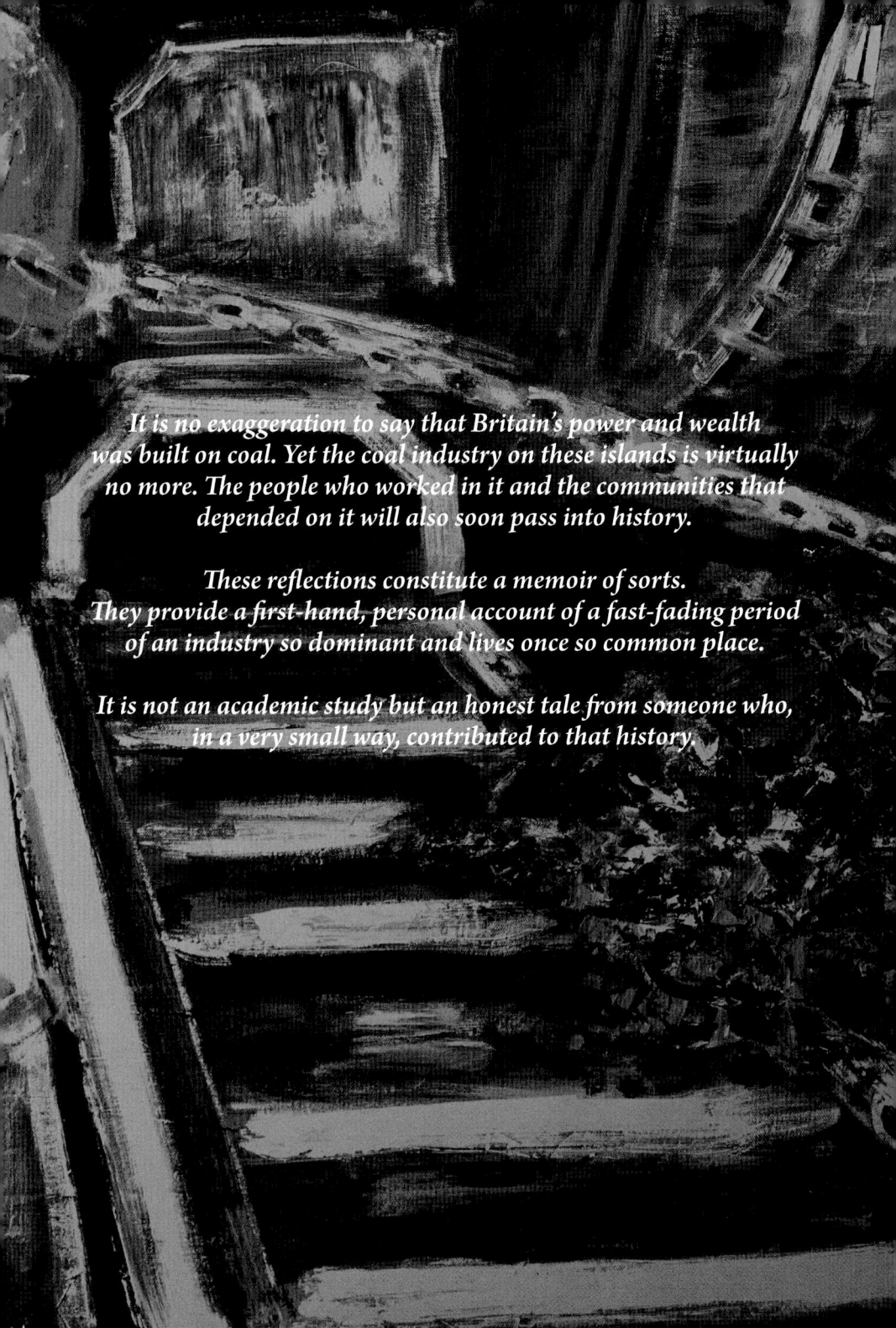

It is no exaggeration to say that Britain's power and wealth was built on coal. Yet the coal industry on these islands is virtually no more. The people who worked in it and the communities that depended on it will also soon pass into history.

These reflections constitute a memoir of sorts. They provide a first-hand, personal account of a fast-fading period of an industry so dominant and lives once so common place.

It is not an academic study but an honest tale from someone who, in a very small way, contributed to that history.